DAWN'S LIGHT

DAWN'S LIGHT

A Journey of Hope and Healing

JADIE HAGER

with David Hager

Dawn's Light – A Journey of Hope and Healing

"No missionary story I have read is more heartrending than the account of the savage attack on the Beebe family in the islands of Palau. But as dark as the story is, the shining light of God's forgiveness manifested through this wonderful family is an even greater testimony. In a day when so many are abused and greatly wronged, the message of Jadie (Beebe) Hager's book is timely and will bring healing and freedom. I highly recommend this book to every believer, especially those who have suffered deep and enduring pain."

—Randy Hurst, Communications Director
Assemblies of God World Missions

"Shortly after the vile attack on her family when Jadie was only eleven, Jadie's parents told their story in the church I then pastored. I have never forgotten what Jadie's missionary dad said that day to our church family: 'The Bible does *not* say "We *feel* that in all things God works for the good." But rather, "We *know* that in all things God is working for the good" (Romans 8:28). Our *knowings* must be deeper than our *feelings*.'

"Now, thirty years later, Jadie shares a riveting account of the violent assault and its aftermath—the journey toward wholeness and forgiveness, the good that God has worked. *Echoes of Darkness* is grounded in biblical truth lived out through experience. I couldn't put her book down. It is a must-read for anyone who has experienced trauma, loss, violence, or injustice, or for anyone who seeks to minister to a loved one with deep physical and/or emotional wounds."

—Dr. George O. Wood, General Superintendent
The General Council of the Assemblies of God

"Though awful and appalling things were done to Jadie and her family while faithfully serving the Lord, Jadie's story is one of victory, not defeat. She writes as a victor, not a victim. Her total trust in the Lord to redeem our heartbreaking experiences is revealed in sentences like this: 'Our life is like clay. Clay that is left to the effects of the environment will become dry, then hard and brittle, eventually becoming useless. Clay that is surrendered to the Potter's hand will be molded and stretched, but finally used for a purpose designed by the Potter.' You'll want to read this book and share it with your friends and family."

—John M. Palmer, President
EMERGE Counseling Services, Akron, Ohio

You, Lord, are my lamp;
the Lord turns my darkness into light.
(2 Samuel 22:29)

But you are a chosen people, a royal priesthood, a holy nation,
God's special possession, that you may declare the praises of him who
called you out of darkness into his wonderful light.
(1 Peter 2:9)

This is the message we have heard from him and declare to you:
God is light; in him there is no darkness at all.
(1 John 1:5)

"For our struggle is not against flesh and blood, but against the
rulers, against the authorities, against the powers of this dark world and
against the spiritual forces of evil in the heavenly realms. Therefore, put
on the full armor of God, so that when the day of evil comes, you may
be able to stand your ground, and after you have
done everything, to stand."
(Ephesians 6:12-13)

X -

CONTENTS

The Heart of the Matter

It is truly the desire of my heart that my story in this book will light the way to restoration and freedom for you, my reader. Whatever you have suffered, or are still suffering, my prayer is that you will be blessed and strengthened through the grace of God as I have been.

This book describes the events of one horrific night when my family and I were attacked by armed intruders who broke into our home on the mission field. It also contains an honest account of the emotional and spiritual issues with which I struggled for years afterward.

This, however, is not a story of tragedy but of victory, much like the life of the apostle Paul. Although he suffered much during his life as an apostle, his story is overwhelmingly one of triumph. I don't define myself as a victim. I never will. I am not defined by the tragedy I suffered as a child. I have chosen not to be a victim but to be more than a conqueror through Christ Jesus living in me and through me.

So let me start by saying that this book is written for anyone who has been hurt. Many of you won't experience the kind of trials I have endured, and some of you have even experienced worse. But it is not about the size of your trial; it is about your response to it. I have seen people whose lives have been destroyed by fairly small problems. I have also seen people go through ordeals I can't even imagine and come out on top of the world.

God has given us the tools to rise above anything the enemy can throw at us in this world. But we need to know what those tools are, we need to know how to use them, and we need to have the vision and determination to see the work through to the end. Whether it was the kids on the playground who teased you, a tragic divorce, sexual abuse, or any other hard circumstance in your life, I fully believe, and am living proof, that God can win any hand! To choose to be defined and restricted in this life based on circumstances, attacks of the enemy, or even your own choices is to let the enemy of your soul win. This is the place where we can be devoured. Instead, let us heed the apostle Peter's advice:

> Be alert and of sober mind. Your enemy the devil prowls around like a roaring lion looking for someone to devour. (1 Pet. 5:8)

That enemy is my target. As you journey with me through the story I am about to share, keep in mind that my willingness to bare the deep things of my heart comes out of this one motivation: To take aim at the one seeking to destroy you and define you in terms God never set; and in doing so, help you find freedom and joy in the Lord who has redeemed you. It is my desire that my story will help set you on a path to freedom in Christ and a life of destiny in him.

Our lives are truly like clay. Clay that is left to the effects of the environment will become dry, then hard and brittle, eventually becoming useless. Clay that is surrendered to the Potter's hand will be molded and stretched, but finally able to be used for a purpose designed by the Potter.

Anyone who has remodeled a kitchen or rebuilt an engine knows it will usually get messier before it gets better, but the end state is greater than the beginning, if we see the process through to the end. That is my goal in this book: To give you the tools to work through your trial, to show you how to use them properly, and to help you obtain a vision for where you are going—a vision strong enough to see you through the process.

My life and my story are so much more than surviving a night of abuse. The restoration I walked through was a choice every step of the way. If at any time I had decided not to yield myself to the leading of the Holy Spirit, my journey would have come to an end. But long ago, I decided that halfway up the mountain was not good enough for me! The tragedy I and my family suffered put me in an extreme place to either practice the principles taught in the Bible or be left to the destructive power of post-traumatic stress disorder.

I do believe that dark night in July 1986 had a part in shaping who I am, but it will never define me. It is my Creator who defines me and shapes my future and my destiny. So, while I agree that circumstances affect us and become a part of who we are, I also believe that even when a choice made by someone else drastically affects our lives, we are still the ones with the final say. What you do with what you have been given is up to you. The Bible tells us that we have been given everything we need for life and godliness (2 Pet. 1:3). To live free or to live in chains is up to you.

A Happy Childhood

"You can pick your friends, but you can't pick your family." That's how the old adage goes. In my case, if I could have picked the perfect family, I would have chosen the one I was born into! I have always thought that I had a great dad, that my mom was awesome, and that I wouldn't trade my older brother for anyone else.

Like many children born into a good home. I lived in a bubble of happiness for the first eleven years of my life, unaware of the harsh reality and evil of the outside world. My parents met at Northwest Bible College then were married right after graduation and started a family. Their hearts' desire was to start a family and be missionaries. Family came first. My dad started working as a youth pastor then an associate pastor. Jeremy and I were both born during this time. In 1979 we moved to Vader, Washington where Dad took a senior pastor position at a small Assemblies of God church. I was four years old at the time and just about to start school and my brother Jeremy was five.

Life was simple and easy for Jeremy and me in Vader. Our home was always full of love, laughter, and warmth. Mom sang God's praises all day long as she cleaned the house and took care of us. Not knowing that brothers and sisters were not supposed to get along (and our parents certainly never mentioned this), Jeremy and I were best friends. We played soccer together and rode our bikes all over town. Later, we learned to ride motorcycles and make mud pies. Life seemed perfect. But before long, the call to missions was strong on my parents' hearts.

During the summer of my eighth birthday, we went to Springfield, Missouri, to attend a missionary training camp. It was a grand adventure for our whole family. We learned all about being missionaries: meeting exotic people, eating strange foods, going to distant lands, and expecting the move of God in the middle of it all. Even as a child, I loved it. Most of all, I loved the idea of sharing the love of God with people who hadn't heard about him.

After the training camp, we were expected to spend the summer traveling around the country, visiting churches, and trying to raise enough monthly support to cover a family of four on the mission field. So, we loaded up all of our earthly goods, crammed them into a footlocker, and strapped it tightly to the top of our little red Chevy Chevette.

We spent each Sunday in different churches, smiling from the front row as Mom and Dad shared their story over and over again. Then there was the "meet and greet" time, usually followed by lunch at the pastor's house. Monday morning we were back on the road. Ninety-nine bottles of pop on the wall. The license plate game. The alphabet game. Highway bingo. We were experts at them all!

After a whole year of traveling and fundraising, we were ready and were assigned to our country—the Solomon Islands. We were ecstatic! The life we had waited so long for was finally about to begin. We went home and packed everything we had and everything we could imagine we might need for the next four years into a large wooden shipping crate. We said good-bye to family and friends and then boarded a plane to the Solomon Islands.

The Adventure Begins

The Solomon Islands are a string of about one thousand islands in the South Pacific. They are truly an island paradise. At that time (back in the 1980s), the islands were largely untouched by the Western world: the people lived in villages and grass huts, and their small family communities grew and produced what they needed to live.

As our plane made its final approach to the Solomon Islands airport, we got the first view of our new home. It looked beautiful from the sky. Island after island stretched out below us. The water had brilliant shades of blue and green with reefs and sandbars visible all around. The islands were green with trees and vegetation.

As we landed, I could feel an air of excitement in my spirit. The plane stopped near the terminal and they wheeled a staircase up to the plane. As we stepped out of the plane and headed down the stairs to the runway as a nice warm breeze blew all around us. The smell of salt water hung in the breeze as it blew in from the ocean. Palm trees lined the runway, and the local workers smiled and waved as they came out to greet our plane. It felt like vacation. Our adventure had begun.

We made our way into the thatched-roof terminal and gathered our luggage. Customs went quickly since ours was the only plane arriving. As we came out the front of the terminal, some of the local missionaries met us. They loaded up our luggage into a European style passenger van and gave us a ride to our new home.

As we bumped along the old dirt roads, my brother and I sat in the back seat, taking it all in. It was beautiful. There were palm trees everywhere with lush vegetation underneath. Through the breaks in the greenery you could see the ocean. There was no trash and although the buildings and homes seemed somewhat simple and primitive, they were well taken care of.

"Here it is," our driver announced as he pulled into our driveway. In front of us was a beautiful little stilt home (most of the homes in the island were built on stilts to provide better airflow and keep the house cool). The stilts were one story tall. There was one room on the ground level that was a kind of storage room. On top was a simple, three-bedroom home. Different kinds of fruit trees surrounded the home. It almost looked like a treehouse. It was fun to be up in the trees where I could pick mangos and bananas hanging just out my window. Parrots would land in the windowsills. Beneath the house was a great place to play. It was all open (except for the storage room) and was nice and cool. Dad hung a swing under there and it was like a jungle fort.

The next few days were filled with a mix of chores and exploration. We unpacked our things and began to turn this stilt house into our new home. Familiar pictures went up on the walls, our favorite sheets and blankets went on the beds, toys and games we had not seen for months were placed on the shelves, and the smell of Mom's cooking came floating out of the little kitchen.

The common language of the islands is called "Pidgin English" (or "Solomons Pijin"), an English Creole derived from a mixture of the local dialects (mostly Austronesian) and broken English picked up from British sailors who passed through over the decades. It didn't take long at all for us to learn the language. Life was carefree and easy here. The weekends were spent in different local churches as Dad would preach to the attendees and teach the leaders. Most of the churches did not have buildings, so we would meet out under the trees. The adults would talk and pray, while the kids played all around them. And when it rained, we got wet.

By island custom, it was not proper for girls to wear shorts or pants, so I adjusted to wearing skirts everywhere and even learned to swim in an ankle-length skirt. I preferred to be barefoot and to speak only Pidgin, which I picked up quickly. There was one other Assemblies of God missionary family who lived next door and co-pastored the local church and Bible school with Mom and Dad. They had been there a few years and had four kids, two of which were about the same ages as Jeremy and me.

Between our house and the house of the missionaries next door was a nice little cement swimming pool about ten feet wide and twenty feet long, so Jeremy and I spent part of every day swimming and playing in the water with the other missionary kids. After a while, I joined a local swim team that practiced and competed in a saltwater pool. I held a record for most consistently placing third! (It is probably not important to mention that there were only three of us in my division.)

School on the island was hard at first (I was in fourth grade at the time). There was a community school where all of the local children went. There weren't very many light-skinned kids, and those who were there were Europeans who had been raised in the islands. We were, without a doubt, outcasts. The other kids did not talk with us and pretty much ignored us. We did not stay in that school very long. We tried several other options for school, including a small Seventh-Day Adventist school that would remind you of *Little House on the Prairie*. We finally ended up being homeschooled. My mom set up a homeschool room in our storage room, and she taught us along with six other kids from the other four American families in the area. We became a tight-knit group and did most everything together.

There was one addition to our family during this time, a young woman named Beverly. In her early twenties, Beverly lived on another island but was interested in being mentored by my parents. She wanted to learn all about our family, our God, and our Western ways. Most everything in our home was amazing and magical to Beverly. She had never been in a car and didn't even know how to open the door. She had never seen running water, a washing machine, a stove, or a refrigerator. She loved all the new things around her and was excited to learn about all of our wonderful "boxes" (what she called our various machines).

Every now and again my dad would tease her, and we would all have a laugh. She fell for all of his stories and gags. But she never seemed to get embarrassed. When she realized it was a joke, she would laugh along with us and say that Dad was silly. I remember one day Beverly commented on how skinny we all were, so Dad told her that we had a "box" for that too. "You just climb inside and push the button for the desired weight," he said. "Then, when you climb out, you are skinny!" Believing every word, her eyes were as big as saucers, and she eagerly asked if she could try that machine. Unfortunately, Dad told her, ours was broken right now, and we didn't have the parts to fix it.

Of course, every "Swiss Family Robinson" family needs a parrot! So somewhere along the way, we acquired one. His name was Boss, and he was a black-capped lory. He was my dad's bird mostly, but we all had fun with him. His cage was outside the kitchen window and right at the back door of the house. Dad taught him to say "Hello, Boss," and he learned a few words of his own too.

Since there were four families living so close, we all became one big family and were in and out of one another's houses all day long. It was customary to say "Knock, knock!" and walk right in. Boss heard this all day long from his perch next to the door. Without a doubt, this bird had a sense of humor. He would often hear Mom working in the kitchen, and he would call out, "Knock, knock!" Mom would holler, "Come in!" Then he would do it again. Not realizing it was the bird, she continued to answer until finally she went to the door, wondering why no one was coming in. When she got to the door and didn't find anyone there, Boss threw back his head and laughed at her. This was a fun game that happened again and again. Much more fun for Boss, I'm sure, than my mom!

One day, a scrawny homeless dog dropped off her roly-poly puppy at our front door. He was very cute and cuddly and surprisingly fat compared to his mother. He needed a good home, so it did not take much convincing on our part to get Mom and Dad to agree to keep him. He was so fat we called him Bear, since he looked like a bear cub from behind. Boss liked to play with Bear too. He would whistle and say, "Here Bear, here Bear." Since the voice came from the kitchen, Bear thought surely it meant he would get treats; so he ran as fast as he could around the corner, lost control on the wood floors, and slid across the floor until he came to a stop in a pile against the cabinets. Finding no one in the kitchen to dole out the treats, Bear would look around disappointed, and then Boss would start laughing. Another fun game to watch, unless you were the frustrated dog!

The weather was perfect. It was always about eighty degrees and comfortable – not too dry or too humid. It rained daily in the rainy season, but it was always a warm rain. This brought out the frogs. There were frogs everywhere. In the daylight, we made a habit of looking at our feet as we walked so we wouldn't end up playing the never-ending game of "kick the frog." At night we wore flip-flops so we wouldn't end up squishing one between our toes.

Life was peaceful and easy and always an adventure. If an urge for a quick snack hit, we could walk out the back door and pick a banana, guava, or star fruit any time. Our houses were situated across the runway from the historic Henderson Airfield on Guadalcanal, which was part of the famous battle in World War II and which was still an active runway. We also lived on the edge of a large coconut plantation. If we were with one of the older neighbor kids, we were allowed to explore the plantation, which went on for miles.

The boys had a few motorcycles, so one day we decided to go exploring. Imagine how lucky we felt when we discovered an old war bunker with a stash of old bombs and hand grenades – real, live hand grenades What could be cooler than that to a bunch of kids? We rode home as fast as we could over the potholes and tree roots, bouncing all the way. We grabbed a few gunny sacks and then raced back to the stash. We stuffed our treasures in the bags and then went flying back home. Because I was the smallest, I rode on the back of one of the bikes and held all the loot. We bounced and bumped all the way back home to share our special find with our parents. To our surprise, they were not as excited about it as we thought they would be. Our fathers confiscated our loot, trying to explain how hauling 30-year old grenades with rusty pins over bouncy roads was a bad idea and how it would have been really messy if we had blown up. None-the-less, it had been a fun day and it was still a cool find.

There was a plantation behind our homes that led right down to the beach of Iron Bottom Sound, so named because of all the battleships that sank there during the war. It was a great swimming hole. We loved to free dive, exploring the massive sunken vessels. Many were just off the beach and so shallow that large portions extended up out of the water. One day we were swimming around, climbing up the exposed portions of the ships and then jumping off. It was great fun. But the old rusty hulls were sometimes tricky to navigate; and while I was climbing to the highest point to make my jump, I cut my foot on a piece of the sharp metal. It stung a little, but I steadied myself and made a great jump. I swam back to the ship and pulled myself up. When I looked back, I noticed blood trailing behind me. Apparently, the sharks did too, because they came in close to check us out. I vividly remember how frightened I was as we huddled on top of that ship, baking in the sun, waiting for the sharks to leave and my bleeding to stop. The other kids told me how a shark would go after the blood and likely pick off the smallest, slowest person—me. Fortunately, I had a loyal brother who always stayed by my side. Looking back now, as the mother of four children, I realize just how much freedom we had. The Solomons were seemingly a safe place, and we were free to enjoy them.

There were times when we would travel to other islands so Dad could teach in their Bible schools. The only way to get from one island to the next was by canoe. It was a twenty-two-foot canoe with a small outboard motor. A trip from one island to the next generally took about eight hours or more. It was a lot of fun being out on the water. Dad would point out all kinds of fish and birds. Mom would sing and play games with us. We would stop from time to time to jump out and swim. And on almost every trip, giant pilot whales and dolphins would swim alongside us.

Most of the villages we visited had never seen light-skinned people before, and the villagers seemed to be amazed by us. So they took us in and delighted in sharing their culture with us. They got us to eat some strange foods, such as sea worms, taro root, and roasted rhinoceros beetles. They taught us free diving and spearfishing; and they showed us how to row standing up in dug-out wooden canoes. It took us a while to figure out the balance; but after a good deal of laughing on both sides, we figured it out.

Life on the Water

Life in the South Seas was a wonderful experience for our family. I remember one particular time we had the rare privilege of having visitors from home when my grandma and grandpa came to visit us. I love my grandparents, but they were not the most adventurous of people. We decided to show them the best of the islands and took them to Tavanipupu, which was a private island people could rent for a getaway vacation.

As you imagine this place with me, it is important for you to dismiss any thoughts of a "tropical island paradise." The little island looked like it had not been touched for at least a decade. When you came up to the island there was a long dock where you lashed your boat. At the end of the dock was a small beach. Just up the beach were two tiny thatch huts with no windows and no running water. Between the two huts was a lone fire pit. The rest of the island, about 3-4 acres, was covered with palm trees and bushes. As we stepped out of the canoe onto the dock, both of my parents looked around with surprised faces, as if to say, "What were we thinking bringing the grandparents here?" Jeremy and I, however, thought it was perfect. It looked like a great place to explore. We camped out on the island for a few days. Jeremy and I explored every inch. We all played in the water and even got Grandma Peg to go snorkeling with us.

Before we knew it, it was time to head back home. About two to three hours into our return trip, the skies began to cloud up and the seas began to swell. Dad could tell that we were in for a hard ride, but he never let on to the rest of us. He told Mom to lead us in some songs, and we sang and sang as the waves got higher and higher.

Another hour into the trip, we were riding up and down twelve- to fourteen-foot swells. The front of the canoe launched out into the air as we crested each wave and then fall as we raced down the back of the wave. The little outboard motor screamed as it rose up out of the water and beat against the air for a few seconds before dropping back into the next wave.

We'd drop down into the gully, and then Dad would power us up and into the next wave. What should have been a four-hour trip took us almost twelve hours.

The most entertaining part of the trip was my grandparents. Whenever Grandpa Ed gets nervous, he laughs. When Grandma Peg gets nervous, she calls out (or rather sings out) the name of Jesus in triplets. So for hours on end we rod up and down the waves with Grandma Pet singing, "Jesus, Jesus, Jesus" and Grandpa Ed sat beside her laughing nervously all the way.

Somewhere along the way, the little plug in the bottom of the canoe came out and the canoe began to fill up with water. When Dad noticed it, he quickly plugged the hole as best he could with what he had available—his foot. Yes, he shoved his big toe into the hole, and it did a pretty good job. Between the little bit of water still seeping in around Dad's toe and the larger amounts coming in over the bow as we crashed through the waves, Jeremy and I went to work with small buckets, bailing out whatever we could between the waves.

So, there we were, for over twelve hours: Dad steering us along with his toe in the hole in the boat, Grandpa Ed laughing, Grandma singing "Jesus, Jesus, Jesus," us kids bailing out the water, and Mom leading us in worship songs. I had no idea how serious the situation was. To me, it was just another grand day in a life of adventure, and we were having a blast. Life was full, and we were living out the Great Commission! Even as a child, I felt like part of the ministry. We did everything as a family. I had accepted the Lord when I was five and felt my own personal call to be a missionary as well. I never felt too young to be a part of the ministry, and Mom and Dad allowed us to be as involved as we wanted to be.

Good-Bye, Solomon Islands

Then one day, while we were all playing outside, life took an unexpected turn when a large transport truck full of men pulled into our driveway. Wielding clubs and machetes, they jumped out of the truck and demanded we get our fathers. I didn't think they were there to hurt us, but they did sound angry. My parents came outside and sent Jeremy and me into a back room in our house along with the other kids and their mothers. The men outside yelled at our fathers, and they sounded threatening. We began to pray for what seemed like forever. I knew Mom was scared, but she remained calm and prayed. At eight years old, I did not realize how serious the situation was at the time, but I later learned that these men had fully intended to kill our fathers that day. Only by the grace and the intervention of God were they spared. They were able to talk the men down, and the truck left.

It is important to realize that as safe as the Solomon Islands had always felt to us, these people were only one generation out of cannibalism and there were still cycles of spiritual and social unrest. So it would not have been surprising for them to kill us. Unrest continued in the local church that Dad pastored, and eventually the Assemblies of God decided to pull us and the other missionary family out. We took everything we could and left the rest. We left the kitchen window open so Boss could come and go until he found a new home. Our peaceful paradise disappeared, the change came quickly—and my family was assigned to the island nation of Palau.

It was going to take some effort to make this transition, so my parents put Jeremy and me on a plane unaccompanied back to the States. We were to stay with family and friends for a few weeks while Mom and Dad made the transition to Palau, and then we would meet them there. I cannot imagine what my parents went through as they trusted God with their kids and waved good-bye as our plane lifted off. Our flight was delayed for a day in Fiji due to a hurricane; through a series of ham radio calls, Dad was able to contact a local Fijian pastor who picked us up and took us home to be with his family, whom we had never met. They treated us like royalty for the evening we were there and then took us back to the airport after the storm passed. God watched over us carefully and closely, and I am sure my parents interceded for us a great deal for the many days we were traveling and out of contact with them.

I enjoyed my time back in the good old USA and was thoroughly spoiled by grandparents and friends. What was supposed to be two weeks stretched into nine. Once Mom and Dad made it to Palau, communication was almost nonexistent. There was only one flight per week into Koror, the capital city of Palau. Our house was about forty minutes from the airport. So for weeks on end, my parents met each plane, hoping we would be on it. They waited until every last person disembarked. Then when the pilot and crew got off, they had to accept the reality that we were not on that one. They then had to wait another whole week to meet yet another plane in hopes it would be the one.

The day finally came on July 3, 1986. We arrived in Palau accompanied by Mom's best friend from the States. I know it was July 3 because we crossed the International Date Line on July 2, losing a whole day, my eleventh birthday!

We had a great reunion. My parents took us to the finest resort on the island for a birthday/welcome home celebration dinner. We had more than two months of catching up to do, and I remember how they kept saying they thought we had matured several years in that short time. They had put us on a plane as kids and picked up teenagers. We had a wonderful time reconnecting, reminiscing about our time in the Solomon Islands, and dreaming about our future in Palau. There was a real air of excitement and adventure in our hearts.

However, it was not long until those blue-sky dreams would darken into our worst nightmare.

Attack in Palau

Right from the start, Palau was noticeably different from the Solomon Islands. It is still in the South Pacific, about six hundred miles east of the Philippines, and is a series of rock islands connected by bridges and causeways. Instead of picturesque grass huts and plantations, however, cinder-block buildings and broken-down cars littered the landscape. Although it was not the same kind of paradise as the Solomons, Palau did have its good points. For one, the view from our home was astonishing. The house sat atop a large hill, lush and green. Our backyard overlooked the ocean and stretched for about an acre before it gave way to a steep drop of about a hundred feet down to the water below. From our back deck, you could see across the ocean hundreds of miles and "into next week," as Dad would say.

We lived in a local village, but the houses were far apart and we did not often see our neighbors outside. Unlike the Solomon Islands, Palau was not a safe place—particularly for women—and it was no longer okay for us kids to run around exploring or take off on our own.

Our house was most unusual. It consisted of four tin octagonal pods on the ground level, all surrounded with windows. This is where the kitchen, living room, and Jeremy's and my rooms were. There was another octagonal pod situated on top of and in the middle of the rest that served as an upstairs bedroom where my parents' room was. The house was designed this way for maximum airflow, since there was no air conditioning. All the windows had bars on them, which gave the already unusual architecture an unwelcoming feel. To add to this eerie feeling, house was mostly empty, with hardwood floors that echoed and felt hollow. Although my parents had been there for six weeks, our container of household items had been detained at port and so we were basically camping.

There were other challenges here as well. The power company had discovered that if they let people have access to power 24/7, they would not pay their bills. As a result, the power authority rationed the access to power. Electricity was only turned on from five to seven in the morning and from three to eight in the evening. So at eight o'clock, it was lights out, whether we wanted it to be that way or not.

Since the soil was mostly red clay, Palauans did not have the ability to grow fresh food; therefore, once a week a shipment of food would come into the island to be sold at market. Many of the things we could pick freely from our backyard in the Solomons were now expensive and considered a luxury.

Fortunately, I had a brother who was my best friend, because after three weeks I had yet to make a friend. The language was different, the landscape was different, the ministry was different, and I found myself homesick for the Solomons. I did find joy in helping with the puppet stage that we dragged behind our truck into the villages to reach out to the local kids. The church we inherited that Dad pastored was small and had no Palauan attendees just a few Filipino families who lived on the island/ Most of my parents' ministry involved trying to reach the native Palauan children and build relationships to earn the trust of their families.

A Storm Brewing

After we had been there for three weeks, Mom's friend (who had accompanied Jeremy and me) headed back home, and we began our first night as a family of four on our new mission field. We were not yet tired when the power went off that night, so we played a game of cards by lantern light at the kitchen table. A storm was rolling in off the ocean, and the wind was beginning to blow all around the house. The wind had a soothing, rhythmic sound, and it cooled off the house as we made our way to bed. My brother's room was directly across the hall from mine, and Mom and Dad stood in the doorway between the two, right at the bottom of the stairway leading up to their room and prayed for us.

" . . . Amen. Good night, you two. Tomorrow we'll go into town for groceries."

"Mom, can I get some green apples if they have them? Oh, and some Doritos? Please?"

"We'll look for them, Jadie. Good night."

"Okay, love you. Good night."

A few hours later, the rain was coming down in torrents and thunder crackled all around like a sonic boom. At one point, our little tin house lit up like a flashbulb as lightning struck the house. We were all instantly awake. Dad hollered down the stairs, "You guys okay?"

Of course, we were. We were tough missionary kids.

About a minute later, a second lightning bolt stuck the house, and the house lit up again as another crack of thunder shook the whole place. This time, both of us "tough missionary kids" raced up the stairs, taking refuge in my parents' bed. As the storm raged all around the house, we sat together, bundled up on the bed, watching the storm and talking and dreaming about our new life in Palau. We discussed the ministry and the vision we all had for this place, and then we prayed together that God would use our family to reach this nation for his glory. We gave him permission to "do whatever it takes."

Little did we know what kind of storm was beginning to rage in the heavenly realms as Satan laid out his plan to destroy this small and seemingly nonthreatening missionary family that dared to pray this kind of prayer.

As the sun rose early the next morning, I awoke to its warm rays and bright light. I sat up in bed feeling a sense of triumph after surviving my first Palauan storm. Storms here had quite a reputation; but now, on the morning after, all fear was gone and the day was as bright and beautiful as it could be. I got dressed and made my way to the kitchen where Mom was fixing breakfast. At the back door lay Lucky, one of the three dogs we inherited when we moved in. (Lucky, however, was a bit of an ironic name since he was a three-legged dog!)

Stepping over Lucky, I slid open the back door and took in the breathtaking sight of the ocean, which was a beautiful shade of turquoise and as smooth as glass. This place did have its glory. As I took a deep breath of the cool morning air, I realized that this was home now, and I decided I could live with that.

We ate quickly, because we were eager to make the thirty-minute trek into town to see what new supplies and goods the supply ship had brought this week. It was a busy day of banking and shopping, gathering what we would need for the next two weeks. We were already getting better at finding our way around, and the place started to seem like home.

When we got back home, Mom and I put away all the stuff we had bought then started cooking dinner while Dad and Jeremy tinkered with the old motorcycle we had inherited from the previous missionaries. When I went outside to let them know dinner was ready, the dogs greeted me excitedly. Both Lucky and Black were old, but Ginny was a bit younger, with much more energy. All were mutts, but they mostly resembled labradors. Lucky was a dark brown, Black was black, and Ginny resembled a golden yellow. Since she loved to fetch and play, she helped to replace Bear, whom we sadly had to leave behind in the Solomon Islands.

After dinner, Jeremy and I tested out the motorcycle. We rode up and down the hills near our house and around the backyard, being careful to avoid the cliff with the drop "into next week." The hum of the engine brought a few curious kids out of their homes, and we spent the evening finally making friends with our neighbors. All was quiet, and life was getting sweeter every day.

That night, as I laid my head down to rest and breathed in the warm breeze, I thanked God for my family and for the privilege of being a missionary kid. Then I nodded off to sleep.

The Attack

Somewhere around midnight, I woke up to the sound of our dogs barking like crazy outside. Dad hollered down from his bed, "Hey, quiet down, guys!" Finally, frustrated by all the racket, he went down the stairs, half awake, and opened the back door to quiet them. Just as he did, a beer bottle came crashing into the door. It made quite a noise as the glass broke and shattered all over the cement patio. Before he could think, a second bottle hit him in the face and sent him staggering backward. He regained his bearing and slammed and locked the door as bottles began crashing against the house and the barred windows.

A second later he was in my room. He pulled me out of my bed and onto the floor. "Get down and stay low," he said as he gathered Jeremy and me and led us to the stairs that went up to their room. We could hear the sound of whoever was outside trying to bash in the door as Dad pushed us up the stairs.

The dogs were still barking outside. But soon the barking changed to yelping. Then there was one very loud yelp.

"That's Ginny!" I cried.

One last loud yelp and then the barking stopped.

As the crashing and banging continued downstairs, I stared at my mom, terrified but trying to get a hold of the reality of what was going on.

Then the alarm mounted on the stairs began blaring over and over and over again—Dad must have tripped the panic button as we rushed up the stairs. Surely someone would hear the alarm and bring help, I thought. Still so innocent of the capacity for violence and perversion in human beings, I was sure this was all a mistake and within a few minutes Dad would talk to these people and settle whatever misunderstanding this was.

The front door finally caved in under the weight of three men who stormed into the house. I heard Dad yelling at them, trying to stop them as they forced their way in. In the darkness of the night, my ears were like a homing beacon for picking up the violent sounds, blow after blow. Furniture breaking, shouts, bodies slamming into walls, each noise seemed amplified as my brain raced to interpret the sounds so I could produce a picture of the battle and the destruction happening below me. It was hard to know who was getting the worst of it, but the continuing sounds of fighting at least meant Dad was still alive.

Every time I heard him yell, I cringed, thinking it might be his last. I knew they were trying to kill him. Then came a loud cracking sound as one of the attackers took a shotgun and swung it like a baseball bat into my dad's head. It caught him square in the forehead, cracking his head wide open, crushing his sinuses and exposing his brain tissue.

As the men made their way to the stairs, Dad somehow found enough strength to get between them and us again. He fought them about halfway up the stairs. They stabbed him through the hand and a couple more places, and then one of them stabbed him in the side, just below his lung.

Motionless and silent upstairs, the three of us prayed God would deliver us from this nightmare and spare my dad's life.

Dad was outnumbered and severely beaten. A last blow rendered him nearly unconscious. The men dragged him down the stairs and into the laundry room, leaving a trail of blood behind. One of them stayed with him and held a gun to his head, threatening to kill him if he moved or made a sound. He began to cry out in silence to God to protect his family now that he could longer do so himself.

With my dad out of the way and under guard, the other two made their way up the stairs to where we were hiding. As they entered the room, there was a look of evil in their eyes I had never seen before. They grabbed my mom and pulled her away from us, demanding money. When she told them she didn't have any, they began to hit and kick her, still demanding money. Every time she answered that we didn't have any, the beating intensified. When she fell to the ground, they grabbed a handful of her hair and yanked her back up to hit her again.

Huddled in the corner of my parent's bedroom, my brother held me as my body trembled. I was unable to process the scene playing out in the moonlight before me. Mom continued to position herself between us and the two men. When they realized there really was no money, something else appeared in their eyes, and they began to rip off her nightgown. I couldn't bear to watch this, so I turned my head and hid my eyes as I heard them groping her and trying to kiss her.

Knowing full well what they intended to do, she pleaded with them, "Please, not in front of my children, please." She hoped that if they took her away, then they would leave us alone.

During all of this the men would kick or slap Jeremy and I if either of us let out as much as a whimper. Eventually, one of the men grabbed Mom and pulled her away, pushing her down the stairs and out the door. The other one pushed Jeremy and me down the stairs. I did not see where they took my mom, but I could hear the sounds of her struggling as she went.

With both parents gone, I began to realize we were fully at the mercy of our attackers. It didn't take long for me to learn what that meant.

One of the men pulled me into my bedroom, and then he ripped off my pajamas and threw me on the bed. Tears streamed down my face as I helplessly lay there being grossly violated by this man. His long nails tore at my skin, and the smell of beer almost made me vomit as he kissed me and forced himself on me. The tears continued as I tried to fight. Each time I resisted, however, I was severely punished.

Still held at gunpoint in the laundry room, fading in and out of consciousness, Dad could hear everything—especially my desperate cries. Hoping the men would leave me alone if I didn't fight them, he called out to me, "Honey, please try to cooperate." Helpless to do anything else, he prayed without stopping.

When this man was done with me, he ordered me to stay where I was and then he left the room. I thought about making a run for it, but before I could move, the next man appeared in the doorway. Glaring at me with those creepy eyes, he came over to the bed. As the rancid smell of beer overwhelmed me again, I began to shake with fear as I realized that the horror I had just endured was about to happen, all over again.

I was eleven years old.

When he was finished, he pulled me out of my room and threw me into the laundry room, imprisoning me with my dad. This was the first time I saw my father after the beating. The moonlight revealed the gaping wound on his head and his blood-soaked clothes.

Barely conscious, he put his arms around me and exhaled in a whisper, "Honey, I'm so sorry, I'm so sorry."

I trembled in his arms as we both rested in the fact that we were still alive. I found a cloth and held it to his head and his side to try to stop the bleeding. I could hear the men outside barking orders of some kind at my brother. Before long, Jeremy burst into the room holding a ring of keys.

Trembling, he knelt down to us and asked, "Dad, which one is the key to the garage? They want to get in, and I don't know how to open it." In the dark, with blood dripping into his eyes, Dad reached out and felt each key, trying to identify the garage key.

As he settled on one key and held it out, , Jeremy said, "Dad, I only have one chance, and if I get it wrong they will shoot me in the head."

The men had already been playing a game of Russian roulette with him outside. Dad shook his head slightly, uncertain if he had the right key or not, and handed the keys back to Jeremy. Then, as Jeremy was led back outside, Dad and I prayed he had the right key and asked God to spare Jeremy's life. By God's grace, Dad had indeed found the right key and the men got into the garage.

I don't know how much time passed as I sat on the floor next to my dad, leaning against the washing machine and silently praying. I held on tight to his arm, feeling the warmth of the blood dripping from various parts of his body. From time to time, I put my hand on his chest, waiting for it to rise, making sure he was still alive. This was the only peace I had that night. Dad tried to comfort me; but whenever the man outside heard us talking, he opened the door and threatened us again.

Before long, the door flew open again and the third man grabbed me by the arm and yanked me away from my dad. "Now you're mine," he said. He was the biggest of the three and appeared to be the one giving the orders.

He dragged me out of the room and pulled me through the house. In the murky light of the moon, I could see broken furniture and glass everywhere. When we got to the dilapidated old front door, which we never used, mostly because there were no stairs—only a large drop to the ground—the man jumped down and then turned and reached for me. I had no choice but to jump down to him, even as everything in me wanted to run. My mind raced with plans of escape, but I couldn't leave my family. I was afraid to make him angry, because I knew he would kill what was left of my family if I did. As I landed on the ground, he picked up my seventy-five-pound frame and carried me through the rocks and grass.

I hated being carried by him and I felt my stomach turn. I knew his intentions for me. He took me to the hill beside our house. I could still hear the other two men yelling orders at Jeremy off in the distance, relieved to know he was still alive.

When we reached a clearing, the man threw me to the ground. With each man who abused me that night, the pain grew worse. But as he abused me physically like the others, this one also tore at me emotionally. He told me horrific stories of what he had done to my mom. He told me how he planned to murder each member of my family, in grotesque detail. He said he would keep me alive and locked up forever so he could "have fun" with me whenever he wanted.

I was terrified that this could be my future.

It seemed like an eternity with him. When he was finished, he took me back to the house and threw me in my room. Then he went to see what plunder the others had discovered in the garage.

Alone in my room, I fumbled through the drawers in the dark for some clothes. After putting on a pair of overalls and a T-shirt, I began to put on several more layers of clothes, trying to find something I thought might fit my mom. I knew that if we got away, and if we found her, and if she was still alive, she would be cold and would need something to wear.

I peered out the door and saw that the laundry room was unguarded. After looking around, I darted across to find both Jeremy and Dad sitting on the floor. I fell on them in a hug, overjoyed they were both alive. Not knowing if the men would be back soon, we sat quietly and listened as Dad tried to regain his strength.

Then we heard the sound of running water and saw water pooling at the door, running down from above. The attackers had dragged in some hoses from outside to flood the house. We learned later that they came up with this idea from a scene in a horror movie, as a technique to destroy evidence and also muffle the screams of the victims.

The Escape

After waiting for a while in the dark, we decided we had to try to get out of the house before they came back. As the dawn finally began to break, we worked together to find the keys and sneak out through the shadows to the truck. We quickly piled into the front seat. My twelve-year-old brother sat next to Dad so that if Dad passed out, he could take over the driving. We sat for a moment in the truck realizing we needed a plan. We didn't want to leave Mom behind, but we knew that our best chance of finding her was to get help. So, Dad fired up the truck, and we sped down the road in search of aid.

The sun was rising as Dad drove through town, honking the horn and yelling for help out the window. He saw a light on in one window and pulled in front of the house, honking and yelling. The light quickly turned off. Disappointed, we drove away.

As we drove toward town, Dad remembered that there was a US Navy Engineer and Construction base several miles down the road. He was sure they would help us—if we could make it that far without him passing out and wrecking the truck along the way.

In the early morning light, we pulled up to the fence at the entrance of the camp. Dad got out of the car and told Jeremy to keep honking until we saw someone. "We're gonna wake up this whole camp!"

Just then, a couple of guard dogs came charging across the lawn. Dad got back in the truck, and with all the commotion we made, a soldier finally came out to see what was going on. When Dad explained our situation, the soldier opened the gate and ushered us into the camp. We were taken straight to the camp medic. Dad's wounds needed attention, but he refused to receive care until they had examined Jeremy and me.

Another soldier got on the radio and put out a call to the local police. The police organized a search-and-rescue party along with some local volunteers, and they set out looking for Mom. A few hours later, she was found with one of the attackers in an old World War II army bunker not far from our house. She was badly beaten and severely bitten by insects, but she was alive.

The soldiers took the man who was with her into custody, and they helped Mom out of the bunker. One of the volunteers placed his coat around her and ushered her into the safety of a police car. They told her that the rest of us were alive and safe and being attended to at the navy camp.

Dad received the call: "Sir, your wife is alive. We have her in the car . . . and she is singing praises to your God."

The three of us sighed in unison as we thanked God for sparing her life. As we later learned, she rode the whole way in the police car singing, "I love you, Lord, and I lift my voice."

A half hour later when the police car pulled into the camp, we ran out to her. Tears ran down our faces as we were all reunited, with praise and thanksgiving. Mom hugged each one of us and held on tightly as the reality that the nightmare was over and we were all alive began to wash over us in waves. The four of us knelt down together in that moment to thank God for sparing our lives and for bringing us back together again. We asked for his wisdom for the next step and for healing.

Meanwhile the storm was still raging in the heavenly realms as our heavenly Father laid out his plan to restore this small and devastated missionary family, and to reach a nation with his message of redemption and healing power!

The Immediate Aftermath

Together again, we were taken by ambulance to the local hospital, an old medical building left over from World War II. Although meager by American standards, it was the best they had. We were all examined by the doctors and nurses as my mom briefly recounted the story of our attack. I heard her explain to the nurse that I had been raped. Although unfamiliar with the term, I put two and two together to figure out the definition.

The nurse was a gruff woman without much of a bedside manner. She tossed a sheet at me and coldly told me to disrobe. I realized that she was going to examine me. I was already embarrassed and in a lot of pain. She was not very nice or compassionate. I pleaded with Mom to spare me from what was coming. Knowing that I needed medical care, she gently encouraged me to do what the nurse said. So I changed out of my clothes and wrapped up in the sheet, then lay back on the table and began to cry.

The exam itself was excruciating, and the tears streamed down my cheeks. I squeezed Mom's hand each time the nurse found an injury or a tender place. When the exam was over, I quickly dressed and curled my tiny body into a ball in a waiting-room chair. I knew Mom would have to go through the same type of exam, and I prayed for her as my tears continued to silently fall as I waited.

When Mom's exam was over, we were taken back to where Dad was being examined. He was lying in a bed in a room full of other patients. The room looked like something from an old episode of *M.A.S.H.* I held his hand and gently hugged him, trying to avoid the IV line in his arm. He prayed with me and reassured me that I would not have to go through another exam like that and that we were going to be okay.

Mom was making plans as quickly as she could to get us home to the States. Jeremy and I waited by Dad's bed, while Mom rushed around making phone calls.

Dad was wheeled out for X-rays, as we sat and waited. When the doctor shared the results with Mom, he started with the "good news": Dad was still in a state of shock and on adrenaline, which enabled him to be coherent. The stab wound to his side had missed his lung by a fraction of an inch. The bad news was that his sinuses were crushed, his frontal lobe had collapsed, and his brain tissue was torn, which exposed the brain. His wounds were critical and most likely fatal. Soon his body would come out of shock, his brain would begin swelling, and his condition would deteriorate rapidly. He would need to be flown to Hawaii as soon as possible for surgery, but the flight itself could kill him. If he sneezed, he could get an air embolism and die instantly. If he made it to Hawaii alive, then the surgery itself might kill him. The doctor's guess was that he had a 40 percent chance of survival. If he did make it through the surgery, he would most likely be physically and/or mentally disabled. He would possibly live the rest of his life in a vegetative state.

That was not the ray of sunshine Mom was expecting. As the silence hung in the room, we tried to grasp what we had just heard.

The police chief then called and asked the three of us to come to the station and give a report. So we left Dad alone and were escorted to the station. We sat on hard wooden chairs, taking turns recounting to the police the events of the night. This was the first time we had heard each other's accounts of the story and perspectives. There was no time for tears as the police fired questions to us one after another. The officer occasionally paused and offered condolences, but knowing how hard this was for us, he was eager to finish the report and let us leave.

We left the police station and went to the airport to buy our plane tickets. We were fortunate that there happened to be a flight out of Palau in the morning. Dad would travel on a stretcher, accompanied by a nurse. His stretcher would take up six seats, and the nurse would take one. Then we needed three seats for the rest of us. The problem was that the plane was full. They could bump other passengers for my dad and the nurse because he was a medical emergency. But because we were not, they could not bump anyone for us. We would have to wait on standby several days for another flight. There was nothing more we could do, so we bought tickets for Dad and the nurse.

When we knew that it would be several days before the rest of us would be able to leave the country, another wave of fear washed over me. This was not a safe place and now we would be left here without Dad to protect us. Mom tried to be strong for Jeremy and me, but I could tell it was hard for her as well.

After the airport, the police drove us back to the station for a lineup: They had caught the three men and they asked us to identify them. There was no back door to usher us safely in. There was no one-way glass for us to hide behind. We were not even allowed to stay together. We were separated and taken by an officer one by one into a little room with about eight men. We stood face-to-face with the men who had so brutally attacked our family only hours before and identified them to the officers. Chills ran down my spine as I walked out of the room, feeling their eyes cutting me to the bone. There was no question as to their guilt, none of us had any trouble identifying them.

The sun set as we made our way back to the hospital. We said our good-byes to Dad, hoping he would not take a turn for the worse in the night. His head was wrapped with gauze into a cone shape. I kissed his cheek and told him I would see him in the morning.

A missionary friend came to pick us up and tried to make us comfortable in their small home. The three of us insisted on sleeping in the same room.

Mom knew that sleep would come only out of pure exhaustion, and when it did, it would probably be restless and filled with flashbacks. She tried to make us as comfortable as possible, praying over us as we attempted to sleep.

That night seemed to last forever. Each time I closed my eyes, flashes of horror overwhelmed me, and I knew it was the same for Mom and Jeremy. Every time I woke up from the images in my mind, I was terrified to go back to sleep. I tried my best to stay awake, but I was too exhausted physically, mentally, and emotionally. As I drifted off to sleep, the images always returned. When it got to be too much, I woke up again. And so it went all night long. Morning couldn't come soon enough.

When morning did come, we felt just as exhausted as when we first laid down. We got ready as fast as we could and made our way over to the hospital to escort Dad to the airport. We sat outside the ambulance on the tarmac with the other missionaries and a small group of believers from the church who had come to say good-bye. Dad spoke to them with words of encouragement and charged them to carry on with the work of the gospel. He held each of us, and we prayed and sang together in a circle the song "In Moments like These."

> *In moments like these*
> *I sing out a song*
> *I sing out a love song to Jesus*
> *In moments like these*
> *I lift up my hands*
> *I lift up my hands to the Lord*
> *Singing I love you, Lord*
> *Singing I love you, Lord*
> *Singing I love you, Lord, I love you*

Dad's head was still wrapped in the blood-stained gauze, and his eyes were still swollen. We must have been a sight to the tourists headed home from their adventures.

The time came to load the plane. We watched as the nurse wheeled him away, and we stayed watching as the plane taxied down the runway, lifted off, and then disappeared into the sky. A new low came at that point, as we walked to the van that was waiting to take us back into town. We began to sing and held each other as we prayed for God's provision and deliverance. When would we be together again? Would Dad make it through this, or had we just said our last good-bye?

As the van wove through the streets, we could only stare out the windows. Then Jeremy said, "Mom, God just told me Dad won't need surgery."

"That's nice, son," she answered, knowing he didn't understand the extent of Dad's injuries. Nevertheless, we thanked God. We didn't realize that with the release of this statement of faith, healing had already begun for my dad. For us at this point, a glimmer of hope appeared.

Dad knew the prognosis for his condition. So on the flight, he borrowed some paper and a pen and wrote us a letter, not knowing if he would ever see us again.

My darling wife and children,

My heart has never been heavier than it was today as I was forced to leave you in Palau. I want you to know how very proud I am of all of you. We never know what we will have to face, but we can be sure that we will never be alone. Even in the times of darkness, Jesus is with us. I would have done anything to keep you from these past few days. I also want you to know that we are a special family that God desires to use somewhere in a special way.

I am a little over halfway to Hawaii and am very uncertain of what lies ahead for me. I admit that I am scared, but God will see me through. So far the trip has gone well, and I so long for you to be with me. I have never had to face what I as a father have faced this past week. I only wish it would have been different. I have never faced surgery before except when I was with you, my love, in Longview. No matter what the outcome, please know that you are and will always be special to me. I know we don't like to think of the worst, but if it happens, all I can say is you have been the best wife and family that God could have blessed a man with. I also plan to be around and share a special love with you that has developed through this crisis. We remember, growth comes through conflict and growing pains are not easy, but we will grow and we will be victorious.

Sherri, I know you understand that I did what I could do. I know you do. I long at this moment to hold you close and just let the hours pass. I wish I could express how I feel in my heart toward you. You are loved very, very much.

Jeremy, you are my only son. I am so proud of how you stood up under life-threatening times. You are on your way to manhood. I want you to know how much you mean to your mother and me. May you always make us proud of you.

Jadie, honey, Daddy loves you dearly. I long so much to comfort you during this crisis time. Knowing what you went through breaks my heart. The only consolation is that this way you still have a daddy who will do all in his power to live and help you through this time. Remember, Jesus will never leave you. You are God's special child and still his virgin. I love you with all the love in my heart. My life has only been enriched by having you as my wife and children.

All my love, your husband and father

We finally got tickets for a flight two days later. Before we boarded the plane, we received a call from Hawaii. My dad had seen the surgeon. The X-rays from the hospital in Palau had been sent with the nurse, but wanting more recent images, the surgeon had ordered an MRI so he could see more clearly what he needed to do. When he saw the results of the MRI, he compared it to the images taken in Palau. He was amazed to find that my dad's sinuses had been completely restored, along with his frontal lobe and brain tissue. He still had a dent in his skull, but that was all. With two completely different scans in front of him, the surgeon, a good Presbyterian man, declared that Dad had experienced a miracle and that he had been healed.

As Jeremy had said, Dad would not need surgery.

The surgeon gave Dad a choice. He could try to fix the dent in his head or just sew him up as-is. Dad had not eaten for days and was hungry for breakfast. The dent would cause no damage, and Dad figured that if he opted to keep the dent, he would have just enough time for breakfast and a shower before our plane landed. He walked out of the hospital and drove to the airport to pick us up!

Somewhere between Palau and Hawaii, God completely restored my father's fatal head injury. Dad has never suffered a headache or side-effect as result of that injury, to this day!

Light broke through the darkness as we boarded our plane with joy in our hearts and hope soaring. The long flight to Hawaii seemed like it would never end. We could not get there fast enough. We hurried through customs and found Dad there to meet us, clean-shaven, with just a small bandage on his head and an arm full of flowers. This reunion surpassed the last, with shouts of joy and embraces as we celebrated the victory of physical healing. We spent the next week in Hawaii with my dad's sister and some close friends who flew in from the States, trying to debrief and come up with our next step.

With the help of the Assemblies of God missions council, we decided we should go to Akron, Ohio, to receive family counseling from EMERGE Ministries, a Christian counseling facility designed to help families in ministry.

It would be the first step in a long process of healing, one that would last much longer and go much deeper than I could have imagined as an eleven-year-old girl. I was about to plunge deep into the mysteries of the human heart, to face fear as a new and present force in my life, and to discover the God who invites us to freedom through it all.

The Healing Process Begins

We moved to Ohio to begin our time at EMERGE Ministries, another new place. My life had changed, and not just geographically. It seemed like for the first time I was afraid of every shadow and every noise. Normally a confident, almost fearless girl, full of life and energy, I now faced this drastic change like a brick wall right in front of me: Can't go over it; can't go under it; gotta go through it.

There is much from our time at EMERGE that I do not remember. But what I do remember stands out like color pictures in a black-and-white world. I remember the front of the apartment building we stayed in. It was a red-brick, two-story building with small balconies perfectly in line with each other. There was a security fence, with several cars parked inside. There were nice trees surrounding the property. And I remember rain, lots of rain. I'm not sure if it was the time of year, the place, or my state of mind, but I do not remember blue skies, only rain. I remember the stairs and hallway leading to our unit. I remember being glad that the access to our "new home" was inside an enclosed hallway and not accessible from the street. I was thankful it was not on the ground level.

A small, galley-style kitchen was just to the left as you entered the front door. There was a pass-through bar to the eating area that shared space with a hotel-sized living room. Two pull-out couches sat in the living room. On the other side of the living room was a double sliding-glass door. I hated that door, especially at night. Not that bars would have been better (they had not protected us in Palau). But glass, anyone could break that and come right in!

At night, Jeremy took the pull-out couch bed to the glass (he was brave), and I took the one closest to the front door. I didn't like either option, really. We faced each other in an "I'll watch your back, you watch mine" fashion. Then the waiting game would commence. Would we sleep tonight? What kind of night terrors awaited us in the hours to come? Did we dare give in and let our eyes close?

In addition to this, there was the ever-present kitchen chair positioned directly between the beds. This was the night watchman's seat, the "prayer chair." Each night, Mom and Dad rotated shifts and sat guard over us until we fell into a fitful sleep. There were many nights when they never slept in a bed. They kept one hand on each of us in heated battle with the spiritual realm, fighting for our right to sleep peacefully.

When we did finally fall asleep, the night terrors returned and startled us awake again. To our comfort, we always found Mom and Dad right there. I remember crying, shaking, and then sobbing. There were many nights when sleep came only because I was completely exhausted.

When morning arrived at last, it was bittersweet. The joy of surviving one more night was cut short by the feeling of being more exhausted than when I lay down eight hours earlier. Then came the realization that this was a day I had to endure school, counseling, and tears I did not want to cry.

School was likely the only normal part of that time, but I remember only the hallway to my class. It was a typical junior high hall with industrial tile floors, doors every hundred feet, and walls lined with lockers. I remember my school experience like you would recall a dream in that some parts are vivid, some less clear, and some just fail to make sense or seem relevant. I remember standing in front of the class being introduced as the new kid, and I remember going outside for recess. I remember struggling to make friends, which was a new experience for me altogether. If I trust my memory on all this, I would tell you that first day was the only day I went to school that year. But I believe my lack of memories from this time can be explained by what the counselors called "regression."

EMERGE Ministries was right across the street from the apartment complex we lived in, and we were there every day. It was a grand building and seemed to me like a fancy doctor's office. The lobby had a feeling of importance and was ornately decorated. There were big, impressive double doors that opened into a high-ceilinged lobby. There was a large reception desk with a decorative rock display behind it. When we first arrived, the whole staff was waiting to welcome us and take us to our designated counselors. *We must be important,* I thought as I looked around. *We don't have to wait in the waiting area, and everyone here knows our name.*

On that first day, I walked down the blue carpeted hall behind my counselor to her office. I knew she planned to ask me questions about things I did not want to answer—and for that matter, really did not plan to talk about. Instead, I got to finger paint and play with playdough. I found it funny that she did not ask me any questions about Palau. But I was sure it would come. Still, I knew that if I could talk enough about school or anything else I could think of, then I could waste the hour and get out of there without any tears. Day One: score 1 for me, 0 for her!

She didn't give up, though. The rule was that if I talked, she gave me candy at the end of the session. It seemed childish, even to me, but there were no rules about what I could talk about. I was good at talking, and the candy was good. One week later, the scoreboard read 7 for me and 0 for her. It must have been time to change tactics, however, because the next day in the middle of my playdough creation came the big bomb: "Are you scared at night?"

I was not ready for the question. My red and blue playdough looked colorless in my hands. This was not fun anymore. Where was the candy and why wasn't it time to go yet? Gently but steadily the questions kept coming, until my tears started to flow instead of the nonthreatening casual conversation.

Although I don't remember saying anything more after that question, I do remember playing the "waiting game." If I could go an hour without talking, I knew I wouldn't get any candy, but I also wouldn't need a tissue. But the more I tried to hold the memories back, the more they tried to burst through. My counselor finally worked past my facade and got me to face my emotions.

At first, I was so overwhelmed that a switch flipped in my mind and I regressed to the age of a five-year-old child in the way I felt, in the way I thought, and in the way I acted. I still had plenty of fear, but the memories that had been all too real now seemed like a distant nightmare that had happened to someone else. I seemed to be able to push it away. I felt safer. I did not talk. I did not cry.

My counselor handled this well. She suggested my parents overlook my regressive actions and allow me to act like a five-year-old. They took me to a toy store one day and encouraged me to pick out whatever I wanted. That's when I met Wrinkles. A dark-brown stuffed dog puppet with big floppy ears, his face was all wrinkly and he had big black eyes, and he wore a gray striped shirt and blue overalls. Immediately, he was my new best friend.

From that point on, Wrinkles went everywhere with me, and he did all my talking for me. If someone asked me a question, I did not have to answer it: Wrinkles would answer for me. What a relief to have such a faithful friend! Wrinkles never cried, which is probably why I liked him so much. He also had a permanent smile and was never sad.

My memories of counseling are nonexistent after Wrinkles arrived. I have no recollection of this time, how long it lasted, or how I emerged as an eleven-year-old girl again. I do know that it was the commitment of the loving staff at EMERGE and my parents who brought me through.

Back to Palau

After a few months, my dad received a call from government officials in Palau asking our family to return in December of that year for a trial. Palau was in the process of adopting a more Westernized form of government, and this would be a precedent-setting trial for them. After discussions with our counselors and the Assemblies of God Division of

Foreign Missions, we decided we would go back to help them as best we could. This decision brought renewed fear and sleepless nights for me. Returning to the place from which we had barely escaped alive did not seem possible to me.

I have little memory of the trip back to Palau, but what I do remember stands out like vivid flashes in time. I remember that we were under armed guard and that we stayed at a very nice hotel. And I remember being more afraid of the guards than I was comforted by them. They looked too similar to the men who had attacked us.

When we were escorted to the courthouse, I was surprised by the number of people swarming the parking lot. There were large cameras and microphones on long poles at every turn. We were not allowed to be in the courtroom together, because we had to testify separately. A missionary friend went in with each of us and stayed for the entire trial.

Since the prosecutor felt my testimony would be the most powerful since I was so young, they saved my testimony for last. This made it all the worse because I had to wait with dreaded anticipation longer. And as the trial continued, the media attention grew, so by the time my turn came, it was at the height of its craziness. My day finally came; and as we pulled up to the courthouse, the number of cameras and people seemed to have doubled. As we tried to get out of the car, the reporters overwhelmed us, pushing in from every side. Cameras and mics on booms were shoved in my face, and questions were fired at me. Dad scooped me up into his arms as two men made a path for us. He covered me and carried me inside to safety and away from the mob, and that is how my day in court began.

The witness seat was a big, wooden chair that swallowed me up as I tried to sit up tall and appear confident. I was sitting directly in front of my attackers—face-to-face with them. The judge was kind enough to turn my witness chair a little so I did not have to look right at them as I had to recount in graphic detail everything that had occurred that night. I was examined and then cross-examined.

When it was over, I collapsed from exhaustion. I vowed to myself never to tell that story again!

A Vision of Jesus

After the trial, we returned to EMERGE for a few more months. Two main memories stand out from that time. First was picture day at school. What a terrible thing to do to a junior high girl! I had nothing to wear, and I hated my hair. I broke down before school that day as only a preteen girl can. My loving mom must have realized that this day was not important enough to warrant more tears. Instead, she smiled and said, "Put on some jeans and your favorite sweatshirt. You and I are going shopping!"

She might as well have said, "We're going to Disneyland." I felt like I had been paroled. I remember vividly our trip to the Quaker Oats factory, our lunch, the coffee shop we visited afterward, and the funny old-time picture I had taken. That day, Mom put my rainy-day reality on hold and shone a bright ray of sunshine in my life, telling me that I was more important than the plans of the day. It was not uncommon for my parents to make my brother and me feel like we were the only people in the world who mattered. Although I have many memories of special days with them, this one stands out like a flagship. I kept that picture in my room for many years as a memory of it.

The other memory comes from another sleepless night. We were in a motel room, and I was sleeping on the floor. There was a large sliding-glass door and no deadbolt. I could feel the fear in the room like an abyss of blackness. I lay there on the floor with a steady stream of tears silently flooding my pillow. Dad was standing guard that night and I could hear his voice, but it was distant—almost like it came from another realm. He was praying for me, I knew that much, even though the actual words did not register with me.

Then, out of nowhere, it seemed as though a floodlight had been turned on in the room. A vision of Jesus filled my eyes and my thoughts and warmed my heart to the depth of my soul. I said out loud, "Daddy, I see Jesus."

He looked around and asked, "Where? Where is he?"

When I realized Dad couldn't see what I did, I began to describe the scene to him: I saw a beautiful palace, one fit for only the highest of kings. I saw a grand room with a ceiling that must have been a hundred feet high. White pillars lined a massive staircase, and there were three dozen stairs at least. An incredible stone throne sat atop the stairs, and pillars lined each side, rising too high for me to see the top.

Then Jesus himself came into focus. At that moment, it dawned on me that the majestic throne was empty. My attention was immediately drawn to a brilliantly colored royal purple robe, the most brilliant I had ever seen, lying over the right arm of the throne. Jesus was not on the throne. He was not wearing the robe. He was kneeling beside the throne, weeping bitterly and interceding for me. His body was draped with simple white cloth and his tears ran down the stairs.

Then he spoke to me, "I have never left you. I love you, my child. I will not leave this place of intercession for you; you are always on my mind."

A flood of emotion filled my heart. Then, just as quickly as it came, the vision was gone, but the warmth and light remained throughout the night as I slept in the very arms of my king!

After months of counseling, prayer, and family time, we came out the other side. We were stable and healthy again and ready to get back to life.

I learned much during my time at EMERGE and in the years that followed that aided in my recovery. Now that you know the story, I want to shift and begin to share with you the truths and the lessons that God used to transform me from victim into victor.

Journey to Forgiveness

How many of us have heard or even repeated the phrase "Time heals all"? Take it from someone who has been there personally and has counseled countless other people in similar places over the years: That statement could not be further from the truth. Time can make you numb, but expecting time to *heal* you is a trick of the enemy.

So, if time does not heal, then what does? The answer is simple: Forgiveness.

Unforgiveness consumes. It consumes your thoughts and your actions. It grows in your body like a terrible infection. It will rot and destroy every part of your life. As you may have heard, unforgiveness is like drinking poison and thinking it will kill someone else. This poison is different for everyone. For as much pain as the original attack.

It took a number of years for me to learn the value of true forgiveness and what it really means. But once I did, it was life changing.

Knowing Your Enemy

In any battle, it is important to know who your enemy is so you can know where to put your defenses and where to aim your attacks. The battle for forgiveness is no different.

Our Enemy Is the Devil and His Demons in Spiritual Realms

The reality for me is that the men who attacked me were merely pawns. It was the devil and his minions who actually attacked me and my family that night. They did not want the nation of Palau to hear the message of the gospel. They whispered temptations of greed and lust into the ears of three drunken men, who then acted on those temptations. I mentioned previously that one of the men came to one of our crusades in Palau. Twenty years of prison had destroyed him. Sitting there before us all these years later, he was a broken shell of a man who could not even lift his head. The same enemy that attacked us also destroyed him.

Ephesians 6:12 teaches that "our struggle is not against flesh and blood, but against the rulers, against the authorities, against the powers of this dark world and against the spiritual forces of evil in the heavenly realms." That is why we are to put on spiritual armor for a spiritual fight rather than physical armor for a physical fight.

Our Enemy Is Not God

To say that our enemy is not God may seem like a silly thing to say but consider the teaching you may have heard on James 1:2-12.

Consider it pure joy, my brothers and sisters, whenever you face trials of many kinds, because you know that the testing of your faith produces perseverance. Let perseverance finish its work so that you may be mature and complete, not lacking anything. If any of you lacks wisdom, you should ask God, who gives generously to all without finding fault, and it will be given to you. But when you ask, you must believe and not doubt, because the one who doubts is like a wave of the sea, blown and tossed by the wind. That person should not expect to receive anything from the Lord. Such a person is double-minded and unstable in all they do.

Blessed is the one who perseveres under trial because, having stood the test, that person will receive the crown of life that the Lord has promised to those who love him.

I have heard people say from this passage that God brings trials into our lives to test our faith, because he knows that as our faith is tested, we will grow and then he can give us the crown of life. What is wrong with this theology? There are three clear reasons.

First, our God is a good God, a loving Father, a strong tower of protection, a guide to green pastures and still waters. What kind of good parent would purposefully bring hardship on their children to grow their character? In the physical world, we call this abuse. So why do we rationalize it in the spiritual world and attribute it to God as a good thing? This theology gives us a wrong impression of God.

Second, if this theology were true, then why would we want to pray for any trials to be taken away? If the trial was sent by God, then wouldn't we be praying *against* God?

Third, the context of the chapter proves this theology to be wrong. If you keep reading, after explaining some benefits that going through hardship can produce, James makes a point to remind us emphatically that although trials will come in our lives and although we can grow in faith as we persevere through the trials, the trials do not come from God:

When tempted, no one should say, "God is tempting me." For God cannot be tempted by evil, nor does he tempt anyone; but each person is tempted when they are dragged away by their own evil desire and enticed. Then, after desire has conceived, it gives birth to sin; and sin, when it is full-grown, gives birth to death.

Don't be deceived, my dear brothers and sisters. Every good and perfect gift is from above, coming down from the Father of the heavenly lights, who does not change like shifting shadows. He chose to give us birth through the word of truth, that we might be a kind of first fruits of all he created. (James 1:13-18)

Why is this important? Because if we are taught or feel that God in any way brought on this tragedy or even allowed it to happen to teach us something, then there is little chance we will be able to really trust this same God to help us. Some people will put a religious spin on it and act like they understand and appreciate God's "teaching" in their struggle. But I do not believe these people can really trust God on a deeper level. While they may puff up the religion of it, they cannot fake the relationship of it.

How can you run into the arms of an abusive father or God? God does not bring trials or tragedy. They come from our own bad choices and evil temptations or from those of others. They break God's heart. Can they produce good things in us? Yes, but only if we allow God to lead us.

Knowing that God was not my enemy allowed me to run to him and to be completely open with him and allow him to heal my heart. Knowing that the devil was my enemy allowed me to stop fearing men, allowed me to move into forgiveness, and allowed me to focus my battle on the true enemy in the spiritual realms.

Understanding Forgiveness

Recognizing my real enemy allowed me to move closer to forgiveness toward the human men who had given in to the temptation and leading of the real enemy. Yet just because the real enemy is spiritual, this doesn't mean that these men are innocent. They chose to listen to that evil voice and then act on that temptation. There was genuine guilt on their part. Although understanding the spiritual battle behind the scenes helped put everything in perspective for me, there was still a road of forgiveness I had to walk in regard to these men.

To get there, I had to face several wrong ideas about forgiveness. Likely you have also wrestled with these false ideas, so I want to talk about them here. I want to challenge your perspective on what forgiveness means.

Many Christian counselors, using Scripture for support, tell victims of abuse that they need to forgive. Period. For example, in Colossians 3:13, Paul tells us to forgive others as Christ forgave us. However, this verse in Colossians talks about brothers and sisters forgiving one another. What if those who attacked you were not your brothers or sisters? In Matthew 18:22, Jesus says that the number of times we must forgive is seventy times seven. But this again is talking about believers forgiving their brothers or sisters. In Matthew 6:14-15, Jesus tells us that if we do not forgive others their sins, then God will not forgive our sins. This, however, is not a passage about the rules of forgiveness but about setting your heart right and avoiding hypocrisy.

I am not discounting these Scriptures, and I believe that they do hold truth about forgiveness. But they can also be used out of context. What we do not often hear in Christian counseling are Scriptures linking forgiveness to repentance. In 1 John 1:9, we are told that God forgives us our sins if we confess our sins to him. In Acts 2:38, we learn that we are forgiven when we repent in the name of Jesus. In 2 Chronicles 7:14, God promises to forgive his people if they humble themselves, pray, and turn from their sins.

So, if we are to forgive as God forgives, can we require repentance of the one who sinned against us? Or does the Bible teach that God forgives only if we repent but that we have to forgive even if the other person doesn't repent?

I believe that if we look a little deeper, we will find the balance of God's truth. And understanding that balance makes all the difference.

It Is Not Okay

In our culture, if someone does something wrong to you and then says, "I'm sorry," the customary response is "That's okay." In large part, this is what we think forgiveness is, telling the other person that what they did was no big deal and that we are okay with it.

Now, if someone accidentally steps on your foot or bumps into you as they pass through a crowd, then this works. It is truly no big deal.

But if someone really hurts you, especially if it is intentional, then this answer does not fit. It is not "okay" if someone beats up my son. It is not "okay" if someone cusses out my daughter. It is not "okay" if someone abuses me physically or mentally.

But for many of those who have been abused, taken advantage of, or wronged in a significant way, this is what they think forgiveness is, saying that what happened to them was somehow acceptable when they know it was not. For them to try to make that leap goes against everything in them that stands for justice.

Scripture tells us that God is a just God. That is one of his main attributes. Because we are created in his image and have his law on our hearts, there is a part of us that cries out for justice in an unjust world. How then can we witness or experience injustice at the hands of wicked people and because we are Christians feel that we have to completely let them off the hook through forgiveness? (Of course, I'm talking about situations that do not necessarily involve law-breaking, in which case the perpetrator should stand trial in a court of law.)

The answer is that we cannot. Many Christians are told they must do this, and they honestly try. But it then can turn into a warped interpretation of "turn the other cheek" theology. "Go ahead and walk all over me like a doormat. It's okay because I'm a Christian and I have to forgive you!" This kind of forgiveness, however, succeeds only in creating an enormous vault within your heart that is essentially full of dynamite and will one day explode.

This type of forgiveness is not what God asks of us. Making things "okay" is not what forgiveness is about. This is the first roadblock to true forgiveness that most people face. We need to have a right understanding of what forgiveness is and what it is not.

Christian forgiveness is a humble yet honest position that we as children of God choose to take up, where we realize that if we were left to our own sense of justice, then we would not only strike back disproportionately to the abuse but we would also then carry the guilt of having been the instrument of harm. God says that justice is his. He knows that justice comes with a price, and it is a price he paid for us on the cross. While God does not want us to ignore justice, he does want us to turn the mediation of it over to him.

It is much like our legal system. If there is a crime, we are not allowed to act as vigilantes and seek vengeance on our own. No, we call the police and turn the crime and the punishment of the crime over to them. They find the suspects, try them in court, and punish them according to the law. When this happens as it should, the guilty are brought to justice, and the victims of the crime usually feel that some sense of justice has been served and their rights have been respected.

This is what forgiveness is like in the kingdom of God. When we forgive someone when they wrong us personally, we are not saying that what they did was acceptable. We are saying that it was wrong, but we choose not to hold the offense in our own hearts. Instead, we give it to the proper authority (God) to deal with in full justice. We are then relieved of feeling that we need to seek out revenge or justice against the person who wronged us or our loved one.

If you have ever been through a criminal trial or witnessed one, then you know the victim often suffers as much, or more, through the process of the trial as they experienced through the original abuse or offense. Like me in that witness chair, the victim is forced to relive all this pain and suffering. In God's good grace, however, we can be spared the ordeal of the trial process through his path of forgiveness.

But there are people in our society who do not trust the legal system, and they seek their own vigilante justice. They often go too far, and in seeking to right the wrong, they do greater harm to themselves. In the same way, Christians who do not choose to turn their wrongs over to God through forgiveness act as spiritual vigilantes, not trusting God for their vindication and healing; and they often end up carrying spiritual burdens they cannot carry and that ultimately destroy them through bitterness, anger, distrust, and hatred.

This was one of the most important lessons I learned in walking the road to forgiveness. At first, I did feel that if I was to forgive the men who attacked my family, then I was letting them off the hook and they would get away with what they did to us. My need for vengeance and for justice would not let that happen in my heart. Somebody had to pay. The hatred inside me told me that as long as I was cold and hard, then I could stay in control and my understanding of justice would be served. Hatred seemed to give me power. It gave me a (false) sense of security, but it looked and felt like justice to me.

So how do we get past this pain and work through this conflict of the spirit? By not succumbing to those "religious rules" that tell us to forgive because we're Christians but go against the justice we desperately need. Instead, we need to recognize that an injustice was certainly done, while also understanding that God calls us to trust him and to forgive the wrongdoer.

First, God wants us to forgive our brothers and sisters when they come to us and repent. We should realize that none of us is perfect, and we should then restore relationship so we can truly exist as the unified body of Christ in the world. Repentance and forgiveness need to be the hallmarks of the church and therefore a light to the world. For this reason, holding unforgiveness of sin over each other in the body is wrong. However, this did not fit my situation, because the men who attacked me were not believers and they did not repent and ask my forgiveness. So, this was not the best approach for my situation.

Second, if that person does not repent, God does not want us to be eaten up by bitterness and anger. One aspect of forgiveness is not so much forgiving the person of the offense, as it is releasing that forgiveness up to God. In our hearts, we know what happened was wrong and the other person hasn't repented. Therefore, there is no justice in my forgiving them. However, if I hold on to the offense, waiting uselessly for them to repent—this may destroy me. But if I recognize that God is just and if I turn the right of forgiveness or punishment over to him, then I know he will do what is right. This allows us to forgive the person in the court of our hearts and pass the judgment up to God's court.

This was my situation and the approach that allowed me to move into forgiveness.

Forgiveness Is a Process

When someone has really harmed us, forgiveness cannot be a one-time occurrence. We are not able to just say a quick prayer to "turn it over to God" and then move on with our happy lives. "Forgive" is an active verb. It is not something you say. It is something you do. It is a process, not an event. It is a journey, like learning to walk or talk or ride a bike. It is not a simple lesson we learn from a sermon at church or in a counseling session. While you can certainly start your journey at one of those places, there is still more work for you ahead. Otherwise, you may think that forgiveness is merely something you say, which is like thinking that saying "I do" at the altar is all it takes to stay happily married for the rest of your life.

When the disciples asked Jesus how many times they should forgive their brother who sins against them, they had a number in mind that they thought was generous: seven. With Jesus's answer of "seventy times seven," however, he told them that there is no finite number. It is a process that takes time and repetition.

Forgiveness is a choice. If you wait until you feel like forgiving, then you never will. It is not about a feeling; it is about perspective. We do not forgive because we want to or because we feel like it. We forgive because God forgave us and he asks us to do the same for others. And, yes, there is a difference here. God forgives us out of his character of pure love. He balances love and justice in a way that we cannot. We forgive out of love and obedience to our heavenly Father. The other person may not deserve our love, but God does. We therefore trust that as we forgive out of obedience to and relationship with God, he will bring the proper balance of love and justice to those we obediently choose to forgive.

If you forgive other people when they sin against you, your heavenly father will also forgive you. But if you do not forgive others their sins, your Father will not forgive your sins. (Matt. 6:14–15)

Therefore, as God's chosen people, holy and dearly loved, clothe yourselves with compassion, kindness, humility, gentleness and patience. Bear with each other and forgive one another if any of you has a grievance against someone. Forgive as the Lord forgave you. And over all these virtues put on love, which binds them all together in perfect unity. (Col. 3:12–14)

Forgiveness is something we decide to put on, like an article of clothing. I relate this to the countless times I have chosen to put on my gym shoes and walk downstairs to the treadmill. Sometimes I feel like working out. But there are often days when getting on a treadmill is the last thing I want to do. Regardless, I make the choice to put the shoes on and then start walking on the exercise machine. Why? Because I know it is necessary and good for me.

Each time a painful memory arises, you must choose once again to forgive and ask God to give you a new perspective. You continue to take your thoughts captive, making them obedient to Christ (2 Cor. 10:5) and deciding what you will dwell on. You do this until the pain subsides.

Whatever is true, whatever is noble, whatever is right, whatever is pure, whatever is lovely, whatever is admirable—if anything is excellent or praiseworthy—think about such things. (Phil. 4:8)

The memory will never leave. What happened is a part of you and a part of your story. But there will come a time when the memory comes and the pain or hatred is no longer there. This is when you know you have fully forgiven. It is then that your story will be one of victory, and something that can be used as a great testimony to bring hope and freedom to others.

I can do all things through him who gives me strength. (Phil. 4:13)

Forgiveness is what takes you beyond Band-Aid recovery, where the hurt remains but is just covered by man-made protection. If you lift the

Band-Aid, the wound is still there. God does not give Band-Aids. He heals so there is no longer any need for man-made covering.

If you are serious about getting beyond your hurt and truly overcoming this debilitating pain or anger, then you need to take an honest look at what you are doing. Do you want to be more than an overcomer? Then ask yourself if you are succumbing to the notion of being a lifetime victim, or if you are fighting your way to freedom.

As I went through my teen years, the bitterness I harbored made me continually fearful. The night terrors wouldn't abate. I was afraid of darker-skinned people, and I generally felt that others were out to get me. This was not a good place to live.

Like me, you have to reach the point when you realize that you are miserable where you are and that it will stay that way for the rest of your life if you don't do something about it. Your future depends 100 percent on the effort you are willing to put into your healing. It takes discipline and effort. You may say, "But this is hard. It is painful." Yes, it is! But what is the alternative? Living a life consumed by fear and depression or even flashbacks? If you choose not to walk the path of forgiveness, then you choose to stay in your current unhealthy mess.

Sometimes it's surprising how easily a painful memory can be triggered. It can be a smell, a feeling, walking past someone in the grocery store, all of the sudden the suffering comes flooding right back in. Through the years, every time a thought came with pain attached to it, I knew I was still on the journey of healing. I knew that this was one more opportunity to lay my suffering at the feet of my heavenly Father and again make the deliberate choice to forgive and be set free.

When I was about eighteen years old, I finally came to a breaking point. I realized that hatred had been eating me alive and was turning me into someone I didn't want to be. Then I went to God and I released it all. While I don't know how to explain the difference, I knew that this time I was able to fully forgive the men who abused me and turn the justice I sought over to God.

Now when I share my story, I sometimes shed a few tears, because the injustice and reality of the events still touches my emotions. But there is no longer that intensely personal pain, fear, or flashback tied to this memory. The enemy's hold on that is gone. I can honestly say that I am free from that cycle of bitterness and unforgiveness.

Along the journey to forgiveness, you may encounter roadblocks like I did. But every time you choose to get back on the road, you will come closer to your destination - freedom. Somewhere along the path, you will realize the choices you make out of pure determination and trust in God are taking you closer to living freely.

At that point, once you can see where you are going, it gets so much easier. It is like when you see the road sign for your destination saying, "Next Exit," you know you are close! Like a protective scout up ahead, if you allow your spirit and your will to lead the way, then your emotions will naturally follow. But you must drive them and not allow them to drive you.

Forgiveness is the first step on the road to victory.

Unforgiveness Binds the Victim

The truth is that unforgiveness is complete bondage. Through my counselors, through prayer, and through the guidance of my parents, I came to understand that to forgive my attackers did not diminish what they had done to me. When I realized that my continuing to live in unforgiveness and hatred did absolutely nothing to my abusers, it was like a lightbulb went on. I then knew that I was completely powerless to do anything to balance the scales and pay them back for what they did to me. Even if I could have done something, it could never turn back time and undo what had already been done. It would only add fuel to a painful fire.

I slowly began to recognize that my hatred and unforgiveness were making me a scared, prejudiced, bitter, emotionally unstable person without hope. There is no restoration or justice in vengeance and hatred. The enemy will feed you lie after lie to keep you in that place for as long as he can until it destroys your spirit.

As I mentioned, when I was eighteen, this was the turning point for me. My eyes opened to the reality that the only people I was hurting through all my rage and hatred were me and those I cared about, those I was trying to protect. Everything was inside out. That is where the spirit of pretense loves to lay claim to our lives. Pretense is a spirit that says what is, is not, and what is not. It's just like backwards day at school, only we do not set the rules. We get so mixed up we don't know which way is up.

If you have ever been scuba diving, then you know how easy it is to get disoriented underwater. This is a very real danger for divers. If you get in trouble underwater and have to ascend without your air, then you want to be sure you are going up and not down! It is the same when you realize some practical and real truths about forgiveness. Once you realize that unforgiveness blinds you, it becomes clear which way you are headed and which direction you need to head to get back to the surface. In *Forgive and Forget: Healing the Hurts We Don't Deserve*, renowned Christian author Lewis Smedes wrote, "To forgive is to set a prisoner free and discover that the prisoner was you"

Unforgiveness was one challenge I had to confront and overcome. Another serious problem was fear, paralyzing fear personified in the actual manifestation of a dark man in black.

The Man in Black

After our time at EMERGE Ministries was over, my parents felt the call to return to the mission field. After they talked with the mission's director at the headquarters for the Assemblies of God, our family was approved to go to Japan to serve as missionaries to the U.S. Air Force base in Tokyo. I was excited about this new adventure. It was something to look forward to. I had spent enough time looking back. Despite what had happened in Palau, I still felt a call from God to be a missionary. It was good for me to have a new vision, something that directed my focus outward and forward.

So, in 1987 we began to travel around the country again, visiting churches and trying to raise support. Dad bought an old conversion van, and we packed up again and set out. I have no idea how many renditions of "Ninety-Nine Bottles of Pop on the Wall" we sang or how many times we played the license plate game. But the days passed, and we enjoyed being together. It was an adventure again.

This trip was much different from the first time we had raised support. As we traveled from church to church, Mom and Dad now told the story of Palau. They were careful not to share the personal and embarrassing details of the attack, particularly pertaining to us kids, but I could feel the room full of eyes staring at me and the questions circled. Most of the eyes were filled with genuine shock and pity. Some just had a curiosity for more details and information.

After the main service was over, the churches usually broke into Sunday school groups. My parents would go to one of the adult groups, while Jeremy and I went off with the kids. A few times, the leaders of the children's church were some of the ones who were hungry for more of the gruesome details, and they would drill us with very personal questions in front of our peers, relentlessly, until the time was over. We did not tell our parents what happened in these classrooms, because we thought our role as good missionary kids was to support the family. But the shame grew stronger with each encounter.

It was a long time before we told our parents the kinds of questions these people were asking. When we finally did, they put a stop to it. It is funny how we seem to keep our painful secrets from the very people who have the power and authority to free us from them. And we think we are doing it to protect them! That is what shame will do. Secrets we keep from the ones we love are the bricks in the walls of the dungeons we create for ourselves. Truth is the key to demolishing those walls and to our freedom. Shame is the lie that keeps us from recognizing that truth sets us free.

Japan

After eight long months of traveling around and raising support, we had the money we needed to go. We packed up our things, said good-bye to our family, and boarded the plane for Japan. For the first time in a long time, we were hopeful and excited. It was just us again, together. It felt like we were closing a chapter in our lives and starting out again fresh.

In the summer of 1988, we arrived at the air force base in Tokyo and settled in to our new home. Mom was remarkable in how she could take whatever accommodations we had and make a home out of them. By the end of the first day, there were familiar photos and paintings on the walls. Our favorite things were set out, and our suitcases were unpacked. We all sat down to dinner together and thanked God for the blessings in our lives.

The base at Yokota had an excellent American school that all the military kids attended. But because of our denomination's regulations, we were not allowed to attend the base school. Instead, we were required to attend an English-speaking boarding school across town. The traffic in Tokyo was crazy, and it would have taken over four hours to drive to school each day. The shortest and most economical way for us to get to school was to take the train, using Japan's excellent transit system.

Each morning at six, Dad took Jeremy and me to the train station just a few blocks away. He walked us to the platform and waited for the train. Then we said our morning goodbyes and off we went. The morning commute was not bad. People seemed pleasant and professional. Most read the newspaper and drank coffee. The trains did not seem as crowded as they were in the afternoon. It was quiet, and I had a seat.

I had my own space and I felt safe.

The train ride from our home to the stop for the English-speaking school was about an hour, followed by a three-block walk to the school. At the end of the school day, we boarded the afternoon train back home.

This train ride was much different. The cars felt more crowded. Many of the Japanese men drank heavily after work and read pornographic comic books as they rode home. Every now and then, they would look up from their books at me, and my skin would crawl. I could feel their looks and smell the beer on their breath. This opened the door for fear to settle on me, which triggered again those horrible flashbacks.

I did not feel safe.

It was an agonizing ride home. The only comfort I had was my big brother there beside me. But often the train was so full of people bustling in and out that we got separated in the crowd and I was alone. By the time we arrived home, it was late and we still had a lot of homework to complete.

Instead of the happy adventure I had envisioned, I spent much of my time in Japan living with fear.

I remember one time when I came home after staying late at school for an event. I was alone, and the train schedule was different at that time of day. I ended up on the wrong half of a train that split at a certain stop. When the scenery passing by did not look familiar, I decided to get off the train and figure out where I was. Standing alone on a cold, windy platform, I dug through my book bag for a calling card to phone home. When I finally reached my dad, I tried to describe where I was by describing what the symbols looked like around the station. Dad checked the maps and found that I was way off course, and he told me how to get headed back in the right direction. My calling card was running low and began beeping at me, and then the line went dead.

I was cold, tired, and hungry, and it was getting dark. I was scared. The next train was only twenty minutes away. I sat down on the bench and curled myself under my backpack to stay warm. Then next thing I heard was the doors of the train beeping as they closed. I had fallen asleep and missed the train. Now I had to wait another hour for the next one. It was a long hour, as I refused to fall asleep and make the same mistake again. Still cold and hungry, I was also frightened, sitting alone in the dark. Tears streamed down my face as I begged God to protect me and to get me home.

After that night, we had a family meeting in which my parents asked us how things were going and how we were feeling. We wanted to support them. We wanted to be strong. But we also had to be honest, so we told them how we really felt.

They saw the emotional toll this was taking on us. The ministry Mom and Dad were doing at the base in Japan was one of the best they had experienced up to this time. For them, however, they would allow nothing to come before our family. So they made the decision to leave the mission field and return to the States. It would take a few weeks to wrap up everything and head home, but they pulled us out of school immediately and sent us home ahead of them to stay with family until they could join us once again.

Port Angeles

In July 1990, Dad took the job of pastor at a local church in Port Angeles, Washington. My parents chose not to tell the church our story so that we could have a fresh start without our past intruding on it. We bought a house on Lake Sutherland, a water-ski lake about twelve miles outside of town and settled into small-town life in northern

Washington. Mom and Dad thought this would be a great place to relax, have fun as a family, and be far enough out of town to feel safe.

And it was. There are so many good memories from life on that lake. Everything seemed to be pretty normal. Jeremy and I still slept with the lights on, and there were places we avoided and things we chose not to watch. But all in all, life seemed pretty normal. It was my sophomore year of high school and I was fifteen.

It did not take long for me to find my place in the new school. Most of the kids in the school had started kindergarten together, which was intimidating at first but proved to be an advantage because new kids can often be a novelty. I got a clean start, and in my second year of high school I could be confident and look like I had it together.

A Spirit of Fear

Beneath my confident exterior, though, there were still things I had to deal with. Then when I started driving, new issues began to surface. Up until then, my brother drove us into town. I guess I hadn't realized it, but I was rarely ever alone. But at this point, I had cheerleading practice and other after-school activities. Since Jeremy and I were always coming and going at different hours, I bought my own car and began driving myself—which meant for the first time I was spending time alone.

The morning drives into town were normal. It was after dark, as I was driving home alone, when the trouble came, that was when I encountered a presence in my car. It would be a long time before I could tell anyone about him. Highway 101 ran west out of town, passed a lumber mill, curved a bit, and then straightened at the battery shop where the speed limit bumped up to forty-five miles per hour. There was a mile-long straightaway, and then a left-hand curve where the lights from town quickly faded away and the road entered the cover of the thick northern Washington trees for the next twelve miles home. This was the only way home from town.

Almost every night as I applied my foot to the brake to take that turn, I could feel it, or rather, him. The hair on my arms stood up on end, a cold chill ran down my spine, and a rush of fear came over me as I sensed a presence in the back seat. Feeling the chill on the back of my neck, I tried to stare straight ahead. I tried to ignore it, but eventually I had to look in the rearview mirror.

There he was. The man in black, sitting in the middle of my back seat.

I cannot really say it was a man, because there was no face, just the silhouette of a man, dressed in all black with a black brimmed hat.

It did not talk or move. It just sat there, looming for the entire ride home. I could feel its presence. It was an evil spirit, and it was visible.

When it appeared, an incredible heaviness pressed down on me that made it hard to breathe. I did not realize it until much later, but this was a spirit of fear. Every time it appeared, dread overwhelmed me. I tried to fight back, but it only became stronger and stronger. I tried to say the name of Jesus, but no words came out of my mouth. I tried to turn on the Christian radio station, but the radio would not work.

I tried to distract myself by looking out the window; but as I drove along through the darkness, I saw images rolling like film clips against the dark canopy of the trees, images from the past that I had worked so hard to put behind me. I wanted so much to close my eyes and make it go away, but I couldn't because I was driving and had to stay focused as best as I could. I was not in control during most of these encounters, and I often did not remember driving or how I got home. My dad would come out to the driveway after hearing me pull in and find me sitting parked in the driveway in a complete daze.

No one else ever saw the man in black, just me. He followed me for over six months. For the first time in years, I felt overwhelmed by fear again.

I remember lying in my bed at night, almost asleep, when I heard the front door open and close. I heard footsteps coming up the front stairs and then down the hall toward my room. The floor creaked in all the same spots every time. As the footsteps approached my door, I felt a cold, dark presence fill my room. Then there it was, standing at the end of my bed, looking down at me. I don't know how to explain it, but I could see this faceless, dark form staring at me.

I tried to scream for my parents across the hall, but no sound came out. I was totally awake. It was not a dream. I couldn't move my arms or legs. Although I was now a sixteen-year-old lying on my bed in Washington, in my mind I was back in Palau, with the torment that continued mercilessly. These flashbacks began to happen more frequently, each time feeling as real as the original attack.

My parents must have heard me rustling around or groaning, because there were nights when they came in and tried to comfort me. But when they tried to come close to touch me, I fought back thinking they were attacking me.

I tried to combat the fear by memorizing Scripture:

There is no fear in love. But perfect love drives out fear.
(1 John 4:15)

Do not be anxious about anything, but in every situation, by prayer and petition, with thanksgiving, present your requests to God. (Phil. 4:6)

The Spirit you received does not make you slaves, so that you live in fear again; rather, the Spirit you received brought about your adoption to sonship. And by him we cry, "*Abba*, Father." (Rom. 8:15)

I knew there was power in Jesus' name. I had heard that for years in church. But none of this helped. I still lived in fear. When the flashbacks came or when the man in black appeared, nothing worked. The Scriptures did not work. The name of Jesus did not work. I was frozen.

I know others have also experienced this and many who gave up at this point. They tried God's way and it did not work. This, however, was not an option for me. There was something more. There was another step, another lesson I had to learn that would give power to everything I knew about fear.

I had to learn about my authority in Christ.

Stepping into Your Authority

I want to start this chapter with a note on faith, because I believe that faith and authority go together. I have heard speakers talk on the importance of faith and the need to work up our faith; and that without faith, it is impossible to please God, yet with faith we can move mountains. But what actually is "faith"? The definition is usually left hanging there, and instead we find clichés. It is just faith. You just have to have faith. It is a blind leap. It is just believing that God can . . . (fill in the blank). You have to "press in." You can't overthink it. You have to let go and let God. It's that invisible "stuff" we all need more of—and so on.

Somehow, we have separated faith from understanding. It is almost seen as undermining faith if we try to think about it or reason it out. On my wall at home I have a plaque that reads: *Faith is not believing that God can; it is knowing that He will*. One of the main chapters on faith in the Bible is Hebrews 11, which provides a definition in the very first verse. "Now faith is confidence in what we hope for and assurance of what we do not see."

The word 'confidence' is translated from the Greek word hypóstasis, which is a compound word from the words hypó, which means 'to stand' and hístēmi, which means 'under' and is generally a legal term meaning to stand under the legal authority of a title or deed. It means to have a legal claim to something. Where does this legal claim come from? It comes from the Word of God. As we read the Bible, we grow in our understanding of the promises of God and the truths of his Kingdom.

The more we understand and believe these truths, the more confidently we can lay legal claim to them in the spirit.

The word for hope is a confident expectation, not a wistful kind of hope.

The word 'assurance' is translated from the Greek word elegchó which means a proof or test, a means by which something is tested or proven. In this case, it is a means by which the spiritual reality (things not seen) is proven.

So, when we put it all together, faith is when we confidently believe the legal claim we have (as co-heirs with Christ) for the things of the Kingdom (healing, deliverance, freedom) and fully expect them to manifest in our lives, thus proving the reality and power of God's Kingdom in the spiritual (unseen) realm all around us.

That is so much more powerful than just blindly hoping for things we don't see or understand.

Now we can see why it is impossible to please God without faith. Because faith means understanding God's word and believing it enough to take action and put it into practice. God wants us to believe him and do what he says. That is what pleases him.

So understanding is a big key to faith. Understanding leads to more confident belief. When we understand how the kingdom works, then we learn how to operate more powerfully within it. As we operate within the kingdom according to the legal rules of the kingdom, as laid out in the Word, it will result in evidence of the kingdom being manifest around us. This evidence, in turn, will reinforce and deepen our understanding and expectation, leading to even more action and more resulting evidence.

Ok that is one verse. We don't build a theology off one verse. So here are some more verses that correlate faith to understanding.

In Matthew 16, the disciples are wondering what Jesus meant when he said, "Be on your guard against the yeast of the Pharisees and Sadducees" (v. 6). "It is because we didn't bring any bread," they assume because they did indeed forget to bring along some bread. In verse 8, Jesus interrupts them saying, "You of *little faith*, why are you talking among yourselves about having no bread? Do you still not *understand*?" Then he reminded them of the miracle of the feeding of the five thousand with five loaves as well as the seven loaves for four thousand. He had to clarify here that he meant to guard themselves "against the teaching of the Pharisees and Sadducees" (v. 12). In this case, he did not tell them to just believe; he explained to them so they would understand.

In Luke 12:22-31, we find Jesus teaching the people not to worry but to trust God to provide for their needs. In verse 28, he says, "If that is how God clothes the grass of the field, which is here today and tomorrow is thrown into the fire, how much more will he clothe you, you of little faith!" He was trying to counter their lack of faith by explaining the reality and truth of the kingdom to them.

Who is the one person Jesus said has greater faith than anyone he had encountered in all of Israel? It was the Roman centurion who came to Jesus to have his servant healed (see Luke 7:1-10). When Jesus got up to go with him, the centurion told Jesus that he did not need to come to his home. To paraphrase: "I understand how it works. I understand authority. I have the authority of Caesar behind me. I have soldiers under me. Because of this, I tell my soldiers what to do and they do it. You have the same authority in the spiritual realm. All you have to do is say the word and my servant will be healed." The centurion did not say, "Jesus, I just believe you can." Instead, he displayed his understanding of how the spiritual kingdom operates in logical terms and he applied it appropriately. This is what Jesus called "great faith."

So how do we gain understanding and grow in our faith? It is clearly spelled out in Romans 10:17 where Paul says that "faith comes from hearing, and hearing from the word of God." The more you study the Bible, the more the Holy Spirit will grow your understanding the legal rights and authority you have in the Kingdom. The more you understand, the more you can apply. Then as you apply this understanding, you will experience the kingdom operating in your life: you will begin to see evidence in the physical realm of the understanding you are applying in the spiritual realm. Then, faith will come alive.

So, what does the Bible teach us about our authority that we need to understand?

1. There are evil spirits called demons who war against us.

> For our struggle is not against flesh and blood, but against the rulers, against the authorities, against the powers of this dark world and against the spiritual forces of evil in the heavenly realms. (Eph. 6:11)

2. But the devil and his demons are no longer in authority over this world.

> "I saw Satan fall like lightning from heaven." (Luke 10:18)

3. In fact, the devil himself and all of his demons have been disarmed.

> And having disarmed the powers and authorities, he made a public spectacle of them, triumphing over them by the cross. (Col. 2:15)

4. The church is now the authority over the enemy in this world.

It started with the apostles:

> [Jesus] called his twelve disciples to him and gave them authority to drive out evil spirits and to heal every disease and sickness. (Luke 10:1)

> "As you go, preach this message: 'The kingdom of heaven is near.' Heal the sick, raise the dead, cleanse those who have leprosy, drive out demons." (Luke 10:7-8)

It was given to the church at the Great Commission:

> And I tell you that you are Peter, and on this rock I will build my church, and the gates of Hades will not overcome it. I will give you the keys of the kingdom of heaven; whatever you bind on earth will be bound in heaven, and whatever you loose on earth will be loosed in heaven." (Matt.16:18-19)

> Then Jesus came to them and said, "All authority in heaven and on earth has been given to me. Therefore go and make disciples of all nations, baptizing them in the name of the Father and of the Son and of the Holy Spirit, and teaching them to obey everything I have commanded you. And surely I am with you always, to the very end of the age." (Matt. 28:18-19)

> And God raised us up with Christ and seated us with him in heavenly realms in Christ Jesus. (Eph. 2:6)

5. We, as Christians, have weapons.

> For the weapons of our warfare are not carnal but mighty in god for pulling down strongholds, casting down arguments and every high thing that exalts itself against the knowledge of God, bringing every thought into captivity to the obedience of Christ. (2 Cor. 10:4-5)

6. There are angels sent to fight for us against the demons.

The Roman centurion understood that at the word of Jesus angels would be sent forth to do whatever he commanded. This is why the centurion said in Romans 8:9, "For I myself am a man under authority, with soldiers under me. I tell this one, 'Go,' and he goes; and that one, 'Come,' and he comes. I say to my servant, 'Do this,' and he does it.". The Centurion explains in detail that because he understands how it works in the physical with his servants, he also understands how it works in the spiritual with Jesus' servants, the angels. The faith of the centurion was tied to his understanding that Jesus did not need to come physically to his home to heal his servant, but if Jesus were to just say the word, or give the order, that in the spiritual realm an angel would be sent to complete the order, just as he, the centurion, would give an order and one of his servants would be sent to complete it.

Revelation 12 says that it was Michael and the angels who kicked Satan and his demons out of heaven. This means that Michael and the angels are stronger than Satan himself.

> Then war broke out in heaven. Michael and his angels fought against the dragon, and the dragon and his angels fought back. But he was not strong enough, and they lost their place in heaven. The great dragon was hurled down, that ancient serpent called the devil, or Satan, who leads the whole world astray. He was hurled to the earth, and his angels with him. (Rev. 12:7-9)

Let me expand on all of this. Demons are not just creatures in movies. Nor do they come only to torment the evil people of this world. Jesus regularly cast demons out of people, as did the apostles. Paul refers to demons often and to the battle we have with them. The passage from Ephesians 6:11 is the Bible's clearest presentation of the reality of the fight that we, as Christians, have on a daily basis with demons.

If you travel much internationally, then you know that there are many people in the world who believe in evil spirits and experience them in very real ways on a daily basis. We see many exorcisms overseas, but we rarely see it in the West. Is this because demonic activity is not as prevalent in the Western world? Not at all! We are merely insensitive or even blind to their existence.

Anyone who understands warfare knows that the best possible tactic for winning a war is to secretly infiltrate the enemy camp. Ignorance of the reality of the demonic is Satan's greatest tool in the West. Do not be fooled: demons are quite real and active today.

In John 8:44, Jesus calls Satan the "father of lies." He and his demons lie to us and deceive us in any way possible to keep us from coming to know God in the first place. But if we do enter into a relationship with God, the demons still do not leave us alone and then move on. They usually intensify their efforts in an attempt to drag us away from God. Or they will do all they can to keep us from walking the Christian life in power and victory, so that even though we have become Christians, we will not be effective in bringing anyone else into God's kingdom.

The response of many people to all this might be fear. Television and movies train us to be afraid of demons, and so we think they can do all kinds of horrible things to us. The truth is that if we as Christians learn to walk in the power and authority of our salvation in Christ, then demons have little to no power over us. In fact, we are in a position to completely defeat them! We need to unlearn what we have learned and understand that spiritual warfare is all about how we handle the devil.

There are two kingdoms on earth: the kingdom of God and the kingdom of the devil. But these are not two equal kingdoms, and you need to understand that you are on the powerful side of the kingdom split!

In Romans 6 and 8, Paul says that it is our choice which kingdom we allow to rule over us:

> Don't you know that when you offer yourselves to someone as obedient slaves, you are slaves of the one you obey, whether you are slaves to sin, which leads to death, or to obedience, which leads to righteousness? (Rom. 6:16)

There are two ways to handle the devil and his attacks. The first way is to run and hide in fear, giving the demons the power to rule over you. The second way is to stand and fight in the power given you and overcome the attacks of the enemy.

What did the apostle John say was one aspect of Jesus' mission on this earth? To destroy the works of the devil.

The one who does what is sinful is of the devil, because the devil has been sinning from the beginning. The reason the Son of God appeared was to destroy the devil's work. (1 John 3:8)

Jesus' mission on earth was militaristic in the spiritual realms, and he gathered around him those who would help in this work. Then, when Jesus was about to leave this world, he prayed to the Father and passed his mission on to them:

"I am coming to you now, but I say these things while I am still in the world, so that they may have the full measure of my joy within them. I have given them your word and the world has hated them, for they are not of the world any more than I am of the world. My prayer is not that you take them out of the world but that you protect them from the evil one. They are not of the world, even as I am not of it. Sanctify them by the truth; your word is truth. As you sent me into the world, I have sent them into the world. For them I sanctify myself, that they too may be truly sanctified." (John 17:13–19)

When Jesus defined his own ministry, and when Peter and Paul later defined it, the casting out of demons was an integral part of that mission. Jesus came to contend against the enemy and set the captives of the enemy free.

When Jesus began to send out his disciples two by two, part of their assignment was coming against the enemy. First, he sent out the Twelve:

He called his twelve disciples to him and gave them authority to drive out impure spirits and to heal every disease and sickness. (Matt. 10:1)

Notice that before sending them out at all, he gave them authority over evil spirits. Then he gave them their charge:

"As you go, proclaim this message: 'The kingdom of heaven has come near.' Heal the sick, raise the dead, cleanse those who have leprosy, drive out demons. Freely you have received; freely give." (Matt.10:7–8)

Jesus sent the disciples out with the same mandate to carry out the same ministry with the same authority that he carried. Later, he repeated the process with a much larger group of disciples:

The seventy-two returned with joy and said, "Lord, even the demons submit to us in your name."

He replied, "I saw Satan fall like lightning from heaven. I have given you authority to trample on snakes and scorpions and to overcome all the power of the enemy; nothing will harm you. However, do not rejoice that the spirits submit to you, but rejoice that your names are written in heaven." (Luke 10:17–20)

As a side note, it is easy when learning about our authority over the enemy to become too focused on our power over demons to the point of sensationalizing it. But the balance Jesus brings to the disciples here is critical for us to remember as well. Although it may feel good to experience power over spiritual forces, our focus should never be on the fight against the enemy but on our relationship with the Lord. Our joy, pleasure, and identity are to be in our relationship with God, not in the power we feel flowing out of that relationship. Too many get the cart before the horse in this area.

We are called to attack the enemy of this world in the same manner that Jesus did. We should realize that this was never portrayed in Scripture as something optional. It is not the "Great Suggestion." The war against spiritual forces is something we are commanded to be engaged in. We have been given power over the devil, and we are expected to use it. Soldiers are not enlisted into an army and equipped with weapons so they can sit around and enjoy life at the base. They are expected to engage in the battles they are called to fight. It is not optional. It is not voluntary. When the enemy attacks, they fight. When people are in danger, they fight. When ground must be taken, they fight.

Likewise, we have been enlisted in the army of God. We are not our own; we have been bought with a price. We have been given mighty weapons, and therefore we are expected to be in the fight, defending the people, taking ground, and defeating the enemy.

In this, we need to consider the role of the church as a whole, and the role of each of us as individuals within that whole. We need to fully understand our identity in Christ and walk in it.

Our Identity in Christ

We are children of God in Jesus, coheirs and united with him and his power (Rom. 8:17; Eph. 1:18–23). But too many fail to realize their authority in Christ, or they do not understand or have confidence in this authority. They may have heard a few verses about it, but they have been so overwhelmed by negative words leading to low self-image that the few Scriptures they have heard pale in comparison. They would like to believe in their authority, but life and experience have tipped the scales in favor of the lies of the enemy, who has told them they are worthless, powerless, sinful, stained, unnoticed by God, and unloved.

I want to tip the scales back in your favor. In the same way that you may have been overwhelmed by the enemy's inferiority complex, I want to overwhelm you with what God says about your value, your position, and your authority in Christ. I know I have already used some of these Scriptures, but I want you to see them all together here so you can get the big picture.

Our Nature as the Church

One aspect of the church is that it is supposed to be a military outpost! We are collectively called to be the army of God. When you read Paul's letters and the other writers of the New Testament as they tell us how to be the church, you find that much of their language is militaristic terminology. And much of it is *attack* terminology, not defensive. So, why has much of the church taken a defensive posture against the spiritual forces at work around us?

Let's begin by revisiting Ephesians 6. When we looked at it earlier, it was to highlight the reality of the spiritual battle around us. Now, let's look at what Paul says about our role in that battle.

Finally, *be strong* in the Lord and in his mighty power. *Put on the full armor* of God so that you can *take your stand* against the devil's schemes. For our struggle is not against flesh and blood, but against the rulers, against the authorities, against the powers of this dark world and against the spiritual forces of evil in the heavenly realms. Therefore put on the full armor of God, so that when the day of evil comes, you may be able to *stand your ground*, and after you have done everything, to stand. Stand firm then, with the belt of truth buckled around your waist, with the breastplate of righteousness in place, and with your feet fitted with the readiness that comes from the gospel of peace. In addition to all this, take up the shield of faith, with which you can extinguish all the flaming arrows of the evil one. Take the helmet of salvation and the sword of the Spirit, which is the word of God. And pray in the Spirit on all occasions with all kinds of prayers and requests. With this in mind, be alert and always keep praying for all the Lord's people. (Eph. 6:10–18)

This is not just an isolated passage. There are many others in the New Testament that serve to instruct the church in its call to exercise authority in the fight.

For though we live in the world, we do not *wage war* as the world does. The *weapons we fight with* are not the weapons of the world. On the contrary, they have divine power to *demolish strongholds*. We *demolish arguments* and every pretension that sets itself up against the knowledge of God and we *take every thought captive* and *make it obedient* to Christ. (2 Cor. 10:3–5)

[Jesus] said to them, "*Go* into all the world and preach the gospel to all creation. *Whoever believes* and is baptized will be saved, but whoever does not believe will be condemned. And these signs will accompany those who believe: In my name they will *drive out demons*; they will speak in new tongues; they will pick up snakes with their hands; and when they drink deadly poison it will not hurt them at all; they will place their hands on sick people, and they will get well." (Mark 16:15–18)

Here, Jesus does not say that some can do these things; he says that *whoever believes* will do these things. This is an expectation he has of his church. Are we living up to his explicit expectations as stated here? In reality, few are.

One of Paul's main prayers for the church in Ephesus is that they understand their power and that they are able, therefore, to walk in it:

I pray that the eyes of your heart may be enlightened in order that you may know the hope to which he has called you, *the riches of his glorious inheritance* in his holy people, and his *incomparably great power* for us who believe. *That power is the same as the mighty strength he exerted when he raised Christ from the dead* and seated him at his right hand in the heavenly realms, *far above all rule and authority, power and dominion, and every name that is invoked*, not only in the present age but also in the one to come. And God placed *all things under his feet* and appointed him to be head *over everything* for the church, which is his body, the fullness of him who fills everything in every way. (Eph. 1:18–23)

Likewise, James tells the church that, as we submit ourselves to God, we should also resist the devil.

Submit yourselves, then, to God. *Resist the devil*, and he will flee from you. (James 4:7)

The word for "resist" here is not a passive word; it is an active, aggressive, continuing, military-like resistance. It is aimed at relentlessly attacking the enemy, wearing him down, and eventually forcing him to flee. Think about the *Star Wars* movies you have seen: there is an evil empire and there is a group of freedom fighters called "the Resistance" or "the Rebellion." The Rebellion does not just hide out: it attacks the evil empire strategically, with energy and passion, eventually overthrowing the empire and restoring peace and freedom to the galaxy. This is the idea of *resist* that James is calling us to in spiritual realms.

If the church is so clearly called to be a military outpost full of spiritual warriors resisting the enemy, then why are many churches functioning merely as hospitals? Much of the church is focused only on the sick and wounded, with little focus on the actual fight. Helping the wounded is not wrong, of course; it is indeed one of our roles in the church. Jesus said that is part of why he came (Luke 4:18–19). But we should be balancing our care of the wounded with the battle to stop the oppressor. One way to help those hurt by injustice is to actively stand against injustice and the spirit behind it.

At a military outpost, there is a hospital or infirmary, but the infirmary exists to support the mission; the infirmary is not the mission. We should not spend all our time fixing people. We should give them whatever help they need to get back out there, into the field and into the fight.

Our Nature as Individuals

Once we receive Jesus Christ as our Lord and Savior, we are saved from the kingdom of darkness, we are cleansed of our sinful nature, and we are adopted into the kingdom of heaven. God does not bring us into heaven as damaged goods on which he decided to have pity. The reality is that he loves us. His love is not like how we love our pets and take care of them, or like how we "love our neighbor" and tolerate them. The Bible tells us that God loves us as his own sons and daughters; and when he brings us into his kingdom, it is not as second-class citizens. God raises us up to be full sons and daughters.

Far from being unnoticed and unloved, you are God's child and you are an heir to all he has.

> The Spirit himself testifies with our spirit that we are *God's children*. Now if we are children, then we are heirs, *heirs of God and co-heirs with Christ*, if indeed we share in his sufferings in order that we may also share in his glory. (Rom. 8:16–17)

If you have made Jesus your Savior, then you are no longer stained with sin. You have been made new. You are alive in Christ, meaning that when God looks at you, he does not see your past life and your past mistakes; he sees Jesus in you. He loves you. His mercy has covered your past. He has already promoted you to be a full son or daughter alongside of Jesus.

> But because of his great love for us, God, who is rich in mercy, made us alive with Christ even when we were dead in transgressions —it is by grace you have been saved. And God *raised* us up with Christ and *seated* us with him in the heavenly realms in Christ Jesus. (Eph. 2:4–6)

Notice that this Scripture is written in the past tense. That is, Jesus has already accomplished this in the spiritual realms.

> But when the time had fully come, God sent his Son, born of a woman, born under the law, to redeem those under the law, that we might receive *adoption to sonship*. Because you are sons, God sent the Spirit of his Son into our hearts, the Spirit who calls out, Abba Father. So you are no longer a slave, but *God's child*; and since you are a son, God has made you *also an heir*. (Gal. 4:4–7)

See *what great love the Father has lavished on us*, that we should be called children of God! And that is what we are! (1 John 3:1)

So in Christ Jesus you are all *children of God* through faith. (Gal. 3:26)

He who unites himself with the Lord is one with him in spirit. (1 Cor. 6:17)

Through these he has given us his very great and precious promises, so that through them you may *participate in the divine nature*, having escaped the corruption in the world caused by evil desires. (2 Pet. 1:4)

Let the truth of these verses sink in! We have all of Christ's authority. He gave his disciples his authority when he sent out the Twelve and then the seventy-two. In the garden of Gethsemane, Jesus prayed for his disciples (and us), saying that in the same way he was sent by the Father in power, so he was also sending us out. Then, in the Great Commission, Jesus stated that his authority is the power in which he sends us out. When he said "therefore," it is assumed that his people are going in his authority; because in that day, when a king sent a messenger, the messenger carried the full authority of the king.

Then Jesus came to them and said, "*All authority in heaven and on earth has been given to me. Therefore* go and make disciples of all nations, baptizing them inthe name of the Father and of the Son and of the Holy Spirit, and teaching them to obey everything I have commanded you. And surely I am with you always, to the very end of the age." (Matt. 28:18–20)

Jesus told us that we will do greater things than he did, not just some but anyone who has faith, anyone who believes.

"Very truly I tell you, *whoever believes* in me will do the works I have been doing, and they will do even greater things than these, because I am going to the Father." (John 14:12)

We have power over the devil because his power is already gone. Jesus has disarmed him and released us from captivity.

"When a strong man, fully armed, guards his own house, his possessions are safe. But when someone stronger attacks and overpowers him, he takes away the armor in which the man trusted and divides up his plunder." (Luke 11:21-22)

Meanwhile, we have powerful weapons that are fully capable of destroying the devil's work in our lives. We are supposed to be waging a war, standing our ground, attacking the enemy. Not only do we have strong weapons, but we should also use them and demolish strongholds with them. Again:

We *demolish arguments and every pretension* that sets itself up against the knowledge of God, and we *take captive every thought to make it obedient* to Christ. (2 Cor. 10:5)

These weapons give us power and strength. They are the power of Christ through which we can do all things. "I can do *everything* through him who gives me strength" (Phil. 4:13).

Jesus has given us authority over the devil; but if we do not understand it, believe it, and exercise it, then we will live as if we do not have it. If the devil can deceive us into believing that he has more power and authority than we do, we will then live as if he does and he will dominate our lives. This was my experience with the man in black. The devil deceived me into believing he had more power than I did, so I lived as though he did because I did not understand my authority in Christ.

So, what is our response? We are to engage in war against the devil! We are to take authority in our own life, submit to God, and resist the devil. We are to take authority over our family and our home. Speak to the enemy, give him orders and boundaries. We need to stop praying for God to come deliver us all the time. He gave us the authority in Christ, so we need to understand it, use it, and be forceful with the enemy.

Much of my power over fear and the man in black came when I finally spoke directly to him, telling him I was not afraid of him, telling him that Jesus was stronger in my life, and telling him to leave me.

Please be aware: You will always lose the battle you ignore!

The Name of Jesus

I want to talk about one last aspect about our authority in Christ. As we saw in the Gospel accounts, we have been sent out in the name of Jesus. This is *huge*, but it is also greatly misunderstood. There are many Scriptures that tell us we have power when we go forth, gather, or pray in Jesus' name. Most Christians I have encountered believe this to mean that there is power when we speak the name of Jesus. If we say "Jesus" at the end of a prayer, then we think there is more power in the prayer; if we say "Jesus" to a demon, then we believe it has to run away; it is like a turbo boost of religious "faith" that we add to our prayers. But that is not what it is about at all. It is not about saying a name; it is about understanding and purposefully wielding the authority behind that name in spiritual realms.

In Hebrew thought, a person's name encompassed their character, worth, reputation, will and authority. This is why when God changed a person's character or destiny, he changed their name. This is why the name of the Lord is a strong tower, because the character of God is that he is a protector of all who run to him. To believe in the name of Christ is to believe in his word, his sacrifice, his salvation, his example, his character and his promises – everything about him.

To go out in the name of someone is to go out in the full authority of everything they are and represent. In the days of Jesus, the phrase "in the name of" was a common phrase used in reference to a king or ruler. Israel was under Roman rule, so it was common for an emissary to be sent out "In the name of Caesar" with the full authority of Caesar and usually with a contingent of Roman soldiers to protect the emissary and enforce Caesar's commands through that person. When this happened, Caesar's authority enforced by the Roman soldiers was to be taken seriously, even fearfully. The people knew they were expected to obey the messenger of Caesar just as if Caesar himself was standing before them. If a Roman soldier came to your door and ordered you to open it "in the name of Caesar," you knew he had the authority and the power behind him to punish you severely if you did not comply.

When Jesus said the phrase "in my name," this is the the reality the people of that day would have understood. When we pray, when we go forth, when we do anything "in the name of Jesus," it is not just a turbo boost at the end of a prayer from saying a name. It is supposed to be a realization that we are on his mission, doing his will, representing his character, in his Spirit, and that we have his authority with a contingent of angels behind us to enforce it.

This is what the Roman centurion who came to Jesus understood. It is what we also need to understand. It is about a position of relationship and authority. First, we recognize that we are under God's authority in the spiritual realm, and as such he gives us authority in the earthly realm. Second, we step into our authority when he sends us out as his emissary. This is what it means to be "in his name."

We are called to be "*in* his name," not just say his name. Jesus did not tell us that when two or three are gathered *saying* his name; he said that when two or three gather *in* his name. If you are saying or doing anything with the spiritual realization that you are doing it under the authority and will of Jesus, then it does not matter whether you actually say his name or not, because you are "in" the name already and everything in the spiritual realm knows that. The only reason we say the words "in Jesus' name" is for the benefit of other people, so that they can understand what we are doing, how we are doing it, and why it is working. If we merely say the word but do not walk in our authority, then there is no power behind our using of the 'name'. Ask the seven sons of Sceva:

> Some Jews who went around driving out evil spirits tried to invoke the name of the Lord Jesus over those who were demon-possessed. They would say, "In the name of the Jesus who Paul preaches, I command you to come out." Seven sons of Sceva, a Jewish chief priest, were doing this. One day the evil spirit answered them, "Jesus I know, and Paul I know about, but who are you?" Then the man who had the evil spirit jumped on them and overpowered them all. He gave them such a beating that they ran out of the house naked and bleeding. (Acts 19:13-16)

Authority in Jesus' name is not a magic word at the end of our prayers. It is an understanding of how the kingdom works, how this authority is structured, and our place in it.

I finally came to understand all of this. I understood that the devil had been thrown from heaven, but I was sitting in heaven now with Christ. I understood that the devil was disarmed, but I had weapons. I understood that if Christ is seated above *all* rulers and authorities, then he is above the devil. I understood that if I am seated with Christ above *all* rulers and authorities, then I am also above the devil. I understood that if Michael and his angels kicked the devil and his demons out of heaven, then the angels are stronger than the devil. I understood that all of these angels, who are stronger than the devil, are sent to serve those who will inherit salvation (Heb. 1:14). So, as I now understood it, the authority structure of the kingdom is like this:

Christ
Believers
Angels
Satan
Demons.

As this sank in, I came to the realization that if I outrank the devil himself by two levels, then why am I afraid of him or his demons? This understanding changed my whole perspective. It changed my life. This is what saved me and what opened the door for me to be able to overcome this paralyzing fear in my life. I came to understand all the Scriptures about fighting fear that I had tried, without success, to use before, but now they had power and were a strong and effective weapon against my enemy.

Overcoming Fear

Fear is a great weapon of the enemy because it causes us to become blind to our authority in Christ. Fear allows the enemy to use our own power and our own minds to control us.

In chapter 5, I started talking about my struggle with fear, with flashbacks, and with the man in black. When the man in black came into my car or my room and I saw him as a man, a physical reality, I was afraid and I was powerless. However, as I began to learn that he was a spirit and that the Spirit of God within me was stronger than him, I allowed the struggle to pass from my physical mind into my spiritual mind and the road to victory began. I learned my authority in Jesus' name. I learned that I could rebuke the spirit in black. I learned I could pray against him. And eventually he stopped coming.

The same was true with my thoughts. When I thought of the actual men in my past, anger, hate, and fear rose up in me. But when I was able to replace these men with thoughts of the demons behind them, then the Spirit of God welled up in me and I was able to rebuke them. It was also easier to forgive the men who were pawns but curse the devil who was behind them. The good news is we are not called to forgive the devil. We can hate him! And we know that he will be punished severely for everything he has done to us.

There are two ways to handle the devil and his attacks. The first is to run and hide in fear. As we have seen, fear is a spirit (and we have not been given a spirit of fear). By giving in to fear, you allow this spirit of fear to rule over you. It is a choice.

The second is to stand and fight in the power God has given you and overcome the attacks of the enemy. As I said before, when we learn to walk in our authority in Christ, we are in a position to defeat the demons in our life. Although knowing our authority gives us the advantage, we still have to fight the battle. Just because the lightbulb goes on, the demons do not run and hide immediately like cockroaches. They will test you and your belief in your authority. Like a stubborn two-year-old, they may not obey the first time. You have to grow in your authority, and you have to make them submit.

When James 4:7 says to resist the devil and he will flee, "resist" is in the present continuous tense. It would better read this way: Keep resisting the devil, and he will flee from you.

Steps (Weapons) to Overcoming Fear

1. Understand That Fear Is a Spirit.
Fear is a spirit of the world, of the enemy, and we have authority over it. The Bible teaches us that this is a spirit that should no longer control the life of a Christian, because we have a spirit of power and love through the Holy Spirit.

> For God did not give us a spirit of timidity, but a spirit of power, of love and of self-discipline. (2 Tim. 1:7)

> For you did not receive a spirit that makes you a slave again to fear, but you received the Spirit of sonship. And by him we cry, *"Abba,* Father." (Rom. 8:15)

2. Make a Conscious Choice to Listen to the Right Voice
We are commanded many times in Scripture not to be anxious or fearful.

> Do not be anxious about anything, but in every situation, by prayer and petition, with thanksgiving, present your requests to God. (Phil. 4:6)

How can we do this? Isn't fear just a natural response? How can we just "not fear"? The answer: By not listening to the spirit that speaks words of fear to us!

When something threatens us, we have two voices from two opposing spirits, speaking to us and trying to get us to follow them. As Christians, we have the gift of the Holy Spirit within us. The Holy Spirit is there to guide you into wisdom, truth, power, and authority through the confidence of God's love and relationship in our lives. If we choose to listen to the Spirit's voice, then the peace of God will fall upon us, we will see the threat for what it is, and we will receive wisdom on how to best handle the situation. Then we will step into our authority as children of God, trusting our Abba Father and out of that framework, we will direct our response to the situation.

If we do not listen to the voice of the Holy Spirit, then the voice of the enemy is there tempting us to react in fear, to run, or to lash out. It is our choice which voice we will listen to. It is our choice which reality we choose. But there are consequences to that decision.

When Moses sent the twelve spies into the Promised Land, ten of them allowed fear to cloud their judgment, and their false report spread panic throughout all of Israel: "We can't attack those people! They're too strong for us!" (Num. 13:31). They chose to listen to the spirit of fear from the enemy instead of the truth of God, which doomed them to wander in the desert for forty years until they had all died out. As the worship song by Becky Fender goes:

Whose report
will you believe?
We shall believe
the report of the Lord!

In the early days of our Christian walk, or in the early days of recovering from tragedy or trauma, the voice of the enemy may be louder. We may have to be intentional about finding and listening to the voice of the Holy Spirit. Or we may have to seek the help of a spiritual mentor or pastor to help us hear God's voice. But, in time, the more we choose to listen to the voice of the Holy Spirit, the easier he is to hear and the easier it becomes to follow his leading. Then we will feel the love and protection of God more strongly and move into the realization of perfect love casting out fear.

3. Build Relationship by Abiding in Christ

We cannot expect to hear the calming voice of God in the moment if we have not taken the time to build that relationship with him throughout the week. We cannot use the truths of Scripture if we do not know them, and we cannot identify God's voice if we do not hear it regularly.

John 15 is an entire chapter about abiding in Christ. Here, Jesus teaches us that we cannot bear fruit if we do not abide in him. But if we do abide in him, talk with him daily, listen to his voice, then we will remain in his love and we will bear fruit in all areas of our lives. This includes when we are fearful. If we abide in his perfect love, then that perfect love casts out fear.

4. Have Intentional Thoughts

Too many people live their lives mostly ignoring prayer, ignoring the reading of the word, and ignoring the voice of the Holy Spirit as a daily spiritual practice. Then when tragedy strikes, they expect to hear God's voice at full volume and with full clarity. Yet the reality is that most people spend the bulk of their time listening to the voice of the world, through the movies and television shows they watch, the music they choose, and the Internet sites they visit. So, when their day of evil comes, the only voice they have trained themselves to hear is the one that will guide them toward the worldly response of fear.

When the enemy attacks, either we can retreat or we can run toward the battle line. Our response will flow out of our preparation. God wants us to be ready for all that comes against us. He calls us to be prepared.

> Be very careful, then, how you live—not as unwise but as wise, making the most of every opportunity, because the days are evil. (Eph. 5:15-16)

The only power Satan has over us is our agreement with him. What does that mean? It means that if he can plant a thought, fear, or temptation in our mind and we agree with that thought, fear, or temptation, then we give him power in that area of our life. For me, he planted the thought/image of a dark man in black that appeared to be both scary and stronger than me. As a young girl, I agreed in my mind that this manifestation was both scary and stronger than me, and it became so. In the same way, if God plants a thought, hope, or dream in our mind and we agree with that thought, hope, or dream, then we give God power in that area of our life. When I agreed that God was stronger in my life than the man in black, he was.

If we can recognize where a thought comes from, then we can take that thought captive. We can agree with the right thoughts from God, and we can disagree with the wrong thoughts from the enemy.

> For though we live in the world, we do not wage war as the world does. The weapons we fight with are not the weapons of the world. On the contrary, they have divine power to demolish strongholds. We demolish arguments and every pretension that sets itself up against the knowledge of God, and we take captive every thought to make it obedient to Christ. (2 Cor. 10:3–5)

If a thought is from the enemy, and we recognize that, then we can replace the enemy's lie with God's truth. When we do that, then the enemy is totally powerless over us in that area. The tricks of the devil that used to work on me do not work anymore, and I am wiser for it.

5. Put on the Armor of God

Finally, be strong in the Lord and in his mighty power. Put on the full armor of God so that you can take your stand against the devil's schemes. For our struggle is not against flesh and blood, but against the rulers, against the authorities, against the powers of this dark world and against the spiritual forces of evil in the heavenly realms. Therefore, put on the full armor of God, so that when the day of evil comes you may be able to stand your ground, and after you have done everything, to stand. (Eph. 6:10–13)

Paul wrote this warning in Ephesians not to bring fear but to help them understand and prepare. One of Satan's best tools against us is fear. All he has to do is plant a thought, and we do the rest. He uses our own minds against us, and the thoughts start rolling:

"There's someone else; my spouse is cheating on me."

"Something bad is about to happen; I can feel it."

"We're going to lose the house and go bankrupt."

"I'm going to get fired; I know it!"

The list goes on and on as we enter a downward spiral of fear. At this point, we have just flung the door wide open for Satan to wreak havoc in our lives.

One afternoon, when my first two sons were about seven and eight years old, they (along with some help from their dad) took a large toy rat and attached a fishing line to it; they strung the fishing line across the floor to the other side of our downstairs game room; and then they placed the rat on the floor just inside the door of our downstairs guest room. Their dad hid across the room, out of sight. Then the boys began to shout excitedly for me to come quick. As I came to the bottom of the stairs, they were pointing toward the guest room and yelling, "It went in there! It went in there!"

Unsure of what the excitement was all about, I crept cautiously toward the door. When I was within a few feet, my husband pulled rapidly on the fishing wire, causing the rat to race across the floor toward me. It chased me as I ran screaming out of the room and halfway up the stairs.

Being a good mother, I stopped halfway up to look back and make sure my two dear children were safe from the horrible creature, only to see them rolling on the floor and laughing hysterically. My eight-year-old was laughing so hard he was crying. Making my way back down the stairs, I saw my seven-year-old giving my husband a big high five as he pulled the hidden video camera out from under a stuffed lion.

They got me. And the following Sunday in church, my husband felt it necessary to play back the video for the whole congregation. But now, I have learned to recognize their tricks, and they are no longer able to "get me" as often as they used to.

Satan is like that. He loves to jump out from around the corner and scare the life out of you. How many times will he do that before you catch on? The first step to defeat the enemy is learning to recognize his tactics and avoid "being got." Then you get to turn the tables on him. When we get to this point, we are in the driver's seat in our lives.

The focus of the Ephesians passage on the armor of God is on being prepared for whatever may come against us so that we will react out of godly preparation and not out of worldly fear.

Good parents prepare their children to avoid the things in life that could hurt them. Have you ever seen a parent warn their children to watch out for cars? That if they run out in the road they could get hit by a car? Why do parents do that? It is not to frighten their children but to warn them of potential harm and to educate them about what can hurt them. Cars drive on the road. There is therefore a simple cause and effect at work here: If you play in the road, you might get hit by a car.

We know the stove is hot. So parents tell their kids not to touch the stove or they will get burned. When my daughter was a year old, I had to follow her all around the house. If I wasn't watching, she would put things in her mouth, stick her fingers in electrical outlets, and play in the toilet. It took a close eye to keep her out of trouble. If I told her no once, would she get it? No, it took about a thousand times.

My kids are older now, and I do not have to worry about them playing in the toilet or putting their finger in an outlet. That is because they have understanding, and they know the dangers of electricity and playing in the road. More often than not, they make choices to avoid those dangers. It is something they have learned by listening to my direction over the years. Likewise, God gives us directives in Scripture that prepare us for the dangers we may face in life. Knowing that giving in to fear and lies will harm us, his word gives us guidance that helps us grow in our understanding and overcome the fear and lies.

Years ago, my boys were really into rollerblades—but boys and wheels can be a dangerous combination! First, wheels on shoes, then wheels on bikes, then scooters, and then cars! When they first started rollerblading, it took twenty minutes to get them dressed. I had to help them put on a helmet, then their wrist guards, gloves, elbow pads, and knee pads, and quite often they stuffed the seat of their pants with a pillow. Why? It was all to protect them. They knew that launching off the driveway on wheels can bring pain. Pain reduces fun; therefore, they figured they would reduce the potential of pain and increase the fun. They were young, but they got the idea. This is the same concept as putting on the armor of God.

When we lived in Indiana, there were some large coyotes in the woods behind our house and I warned my kids to keep an eye out for them. We had a fence, but I was constantly aware of the danger. Because of that danger I prepared them to be alert. It is the same in the spiritual realm. This world is not our own, and Satan roams about like a roaring lion seeking whom he may devour (1 Pet.5:8).

God stresses preparation again and again in the Bible. There are countless Scriptures where he tells us to "ready ourselves." Jesus himself felt the need to be prepared. He often drew away early in the morning to pray. He knew the risks of his chosen life, but he also knew where to seek his strength, guidance, and preparation. My husband is in the military. One lesson you learn in the army is how much our soldiers are trained and prepared for battle, from boot camp onward. It is constant. They are given armor and weapons, and they are well trained in how to use them. If they were not extensively prepared, then they would be set up for failure. Although we know we are in the middle of a spiritual battle in this world, how much do you prepare and train to be successful in this war? Is your armor ready?

In Ephesians 6, Paul tells us how to prepare with the following pieces of "armor":

- *Truth.* Are you meditating on what is true in your life? Are you taking your thoughts captive to Christ? Are you denying the lies of the enemy?
- *Righteousness.* Are you living right before God? Are you avoiding willful sins? Are you pursuing your relationship daily with your God?
- *Gospel of Peace.* Are you secure in your identity in God? Is your heart secure in your walk with God and in God's love for you? Do you deny sin's power over you?
- *Faith.* Do you practice your faith? Do you step out when you feel God is leading you? Do you trust God with your life, your family, your finances, your future? Or do you give in to worry?
- *Salvation.* Are you walking daily in the reality of your salvation? Do you believe you are loved by God just as Christ is loved by him? Have you died to this world and risen with Christ? Do you deny your past's power over you?
- *Scripture.* Do you regularly read your Bible? Do you meditate on the word to the point that it permeates your soul? Do you allow the truths of the word of God to reorder your world and your thoughts?
- *Prayer.* Do you talk with God regularly? Do you share your heart with him? Do you sit quietly and wait for him to answer?

I know there is more depth to these pieces of armor than the little I have mentioned here, but hopefully you get the idea. These are all ways we prepare to be ready for the attacks of the enemy. When we are prepared with truth, the enemy cannot use lies against us in his attack.

When we are prepared through a life of righteousness, the enemy cannot bring doubt of God's love and support in the moment. When we are prepared with peace, we can remain calm in the storm and apply the appropriate defense. When we prepare by walking in faith in the little things, we are quicker to engage faith in the big things. When we are prepared with assurance of our salvation, the enemy cannot use our past against us. When we are prepared by reading the word, we know what the Bible says about the situations we encounter. When we are prepared in prayer, we are tuned to hear God's voice and guidance in our hour of need.

6. Practice Perseverance

Scripture also uses the example of an athlete in competition:

> Do you not know that in a race all the runners run, but only one gets the prize? Run in such a way as to get the prize. (1 Cor. 9:24)

How do you get the prize? You prepare your body through diet and committed training. I would not enter a race right now against a prepared athlete and expect to win. Would you?

In our personal lives, we often worry about our health and try to diet and exercise more. There are just never enough hours in the day to feel like we're in good shape. But when it comes to our spiritual bodies, we tend to be lazy and out of shape and we don't worry about this hindering us in 'the race'. Have you ever wondered what your spiritual body would look like if you stood in front of a mirror? Would you be saggy and flabby or would you be fit and toned? What are you feeding your mind, your ears, your eyes? Is it good, solid, spiritual food? Or do you dine regularly on the junk food of this world and call it entertainment?

I know this list above is not exhaustive. But for me, these were the biggest keys in overcoming fear in my life, and they have worked with many people I have counseled over the years. While we have a choice to enter a physical race, we do not have a choice whether or not to engage in battle spiritually for our lives. Once we are born and start breathing, we are in the battle. The only choice we have is how effective and powerful we are in that battle. Is Satan under your feet, or are you under his?

I believe God never leads us into a battle for which we are not prepared, though sometimes we can walk smack-dab in the middle of a fire we have created. When God leads us into battle, he gives us every opportunity to prepare. Why? Because he wants us to succeed. He does not want us to fail.

"For I know the plans I have for you," declares the Lord, "plans to prosper you and not to harm you, plans to give you hope and a future."(Jer. 29:11)

We know that Satan uses fear to keep us in a place of weakness that allows those fiery darts to pierce through weak armor. We also know that we need to arm ourselves for a battle we cannot escape.

Spiritual Eyes

One of my biggest hopes for my story and for this book is that it may help open the eyes of many to the reality of the spiritual realm in a new way, and for them to see the incredible power that is on their side in a battle where they have previously felt they were outnumbered, unsupported, and destined to fail.

If we understand the spiritual realm, then we can overcome our fear, which will lead to victory in the natural world. We have so many great examples in the Bible of those with solid faith (that is, they understand of the spiritual realm) whose preparation led to victory. First, let us look at David.

David

In 1 Samuel 17, we see the story of David and Goliath. When the entire nation of Israel was paralyzed with fear before Goliath and the Philistines, David alone was unafraid, because he knew the power and the voice of God. David had spent years in the fields with the sheep, praying and learning to hear the voice of God. So when the attack came, David was able to remain composed, know the will of God, understand his authority, and not only face his enemy but prevail. The choice of one boy changed the course of history and changed the position of an entire army from cowardice to victory over the enemy!

When the enemy advances against you, you likewise should not be afraid. Instead, be prepared. As Peter says in his letter, the evil one roams around the earth seeking whom he may devour. He would have devoured the Israelite army had David not been prepared and stood his ground. But God's eyes roam around the earth as well, seeking those who are faithful and through whom God may show himself strong. When the enemy comes in like a raging flood, God will raise up a standard against him. David was that standard!

And then, of course, preparation must move into practice. I was prepared from a young age to have a proper perspective of God and life. I was prepared in knowing my identity in Christ. I was prepared in knowing my authority over the enemy. But when the time came, I had to choose to stand on all that. The enemy was there, standing against me as an eleven-year-old girl and into my teen years, doing all he could to make me doubt everything I thought I knew. It was a struggle in the physical realm to believe what I knew to be true in the spiritual realm.

Over the years, fear has come at me in many different forms. For a long time, it came in the form of flashbacks. Triggered by any number of things, a flashback takes you back to the time and place where you were first hurt and afraid. Fear takes over; and in a flashback, anything you hear and feel can be translated back to that moment in time. In a severe flashback, which I have experienced, there is a danger of your psyche being overwhelmed to the point of not being able to find reality again. Flashbacks take you to a state of absolute helplessness. Whatever you see in your mind, you experience again in that moment. Oftentimes it is a play-by-play of what happened to you originally, but sometimes it changes or even gets worse. Your fears take over; and after many flashbacks, you cannot separate what really happened from the reality of the flashbacks. So the pain or violence you experienced is not just a one-time event. As long as you are a slave to these flashbacks, you will continue to suffer the same horrific experience again and again.

Fear was the source and the fuel of my flashbacks. When I learned to master fear, however, I closed the door on the enemy being able to take me to that place in my mind and torture me.

Looking back again at King David, we see that he was victorious because he looked at the battle with the proper perspective and relied on his years of practice with the armor of God. He placed his trust in the One he knew would deliver him. Then he chose five smooth stones, and he approached the Philistine.

> "Come here," [Goliath] said, "and I'll give your flesh to the birds and the wild animals!"
>
> David said to the Philistine, "You come against me with sword and spear and javelin, but I come against you in the name of the Lord Almighty, the God of the armies of Israel, whom you have defied. This day the Lord will deliver you into my hands, and I'll strike you down and cut off your head. This very day I will give the carcasses of the Philistine army to the birds and the wild animals, and the whole world will know that there is a God in Israel. All those gathered here will know that it is not by sword or spear that the Lord saves; for the battle is the Lord's, and he will give all of you into our hands." (1 Sam. 17:44–47)

The giant roared threats to David to get him to retreat, but David did not fear. He had practiced during all those boring days sitting in the fields watching sheep. How glorious is that? He used his time wisely to prepare, and he always stayed alert, watching out for the enemy that was always looking to devour what was under his care. When a lion came to threaten his flock, he killed the lion. When a bear came to attack, he held his ground. God trained him through these skirmishes so that he was ready when the real battle came.

When David faced Goliath, he did not retreat in fear; he ran quickly and boldly toward the battle lines to meet his enemy. His aim was sure. And with a single stone, he killed the giant. The stronghold was broken. The Philistine army retreated, and the Israelite army surged forward with confidence. In an instant, David's actions moved the army of Israel into a position of victory over the same Philistines that had them cowering in fear for weeks. God did not need an entire army; he needed one boy who believed enough to act.

David needed only one stone to kill his giant, but he was prepared with five. He was ready for whatever came his way. David responded by speaking the truth of God into his situation. As Jesus said, "Then you will know the truth, and the truth will set you free"   (John 8:32).

David walked in a miracle on the brink of disaster. That is faith. There is a thin line between faith and foolishness, but David turned the outcome of the situation. When everyone else lacked courage, his faith turned them to courage. David's confidence was in God, and it was contagious. The Philistine army, on the other hand, had their faith in their giant. When he was defeated, they had to flee.

> Jesus replied, "Truly I tell you, if you have faith and do not doubt, not only can you do what was done to the fig tree, but also you can say to this mountain, 'Go, throw yourself into the sea,' and it will be done. If you believe, you will receive whatever you ask for in prayer." (Matt. 21:21–22)

Elisha

Understanding the spiritual realm will help you overcome fear in the natural. A great example of this is in 2 Kings 6. Elisha the prophet and his servant were in the town of Dothan, and the army of Aram was looking for Elisha to kill him. When the king of Aram found out where Elisha was, he sent horses and chariots and a large force to surround the city by night. In the morning, the servant of Elisha woke up and saw the army surrounding the city. This must have been a formidable sight! He knew the army was there for his master and would probably kill him as well. In the natural world, there was much cause for fear and the servant was afraid, yet Elisha remained calm, without fear in the face of certain death. Why? Because he could see into the reality of the spirit, and he drew courage from what he knew to be true.

When the servant of the man of God got up and went out early the next morning, an army with horses and chariots had surrounded the city. "Oh, my lord, what shall we do?" the servant asked.

"Don't be afraid," the prophet answered. "Those who are with us are more than those who are with them." And Elisha prayed, "Open his eyes, Lord, so that he may see." Then the Lord opened the servant's eyes, and he looked and saw the hills full of horses and chariots of fire all around Elisha. As the enemy came down toward him, Elisha prayed to the Lord, "Strike this army with blindness." So he struck them with blindness, as Elisha had asked. Elisha told them, "This is not the road and this is not the city. Follow me, and I will lead you to the man you are looking for." And he led them to Samaria. After they entered the city, Elisha said, "Lord, open the eyes of these men so they can see." Then the Lord opened their eyes and they looked, and there they were, inside Samaria.

When the king of Israel saw them, he asked Elisha, "Shall I kill them, my father? Shall I kill them?"

"Do not kill them," he answered. "Would you kill those you have captured with your own sword or bow? Set food and water before them so that they may eat and drink and then go back to their master." So he prepared a great feast for them, and after they had finished eating and drinking, he sent them away, and they returned to their master. So the bands from Aram stopped raiding Israel's territory. (2 Kings 6:15–23)

I will bet that when the servant's eyes were opened, his demeanor changed dramatically. Before, he was full of fear. In the natural world, there was no hope at all. But when he saw into the spirit realm, he gained courage. Then, when the army of Aram began to attack, the man of God did not pray out of fear "Lord, please save me," while having little faith that it would happen.

Jesus told us that when we pray we are to believe and not doubt. He said that if we have just a little faith, we can move mountains. But most people when faced with fear will throw up hopeful prayers that have little to no actual faith behind them. This was not the case with Elisha. Elisha understood the kingdom and understood that he stood in the name of God, and therefore the host of heaven had been released to support him. So, when he prayed to the Lord, "Strike these people with blindness," it was with faith, understanding, and boldness.

This is why Jesus commended the Roman centurion as a man of great faith (Matt. 8:5–10). He understood the authority structure in the spiritual realm. Because he was under authority, he had authority over those who were under him in the natural world, just as Jesus did in the spiritual. As a result, in the natural world, the centurion could "say to this one go, and he goes or say to this one come and he comes." In the same way, Jesus could pray or speak with authority, knowing there was a host of heaven around him waiting to put action to his prayers and his commands in the spirit.

We have access to the same power. Jesus has sent us into the world in the same way that God sent him into the world (John 20:21): Jesus was sent with attending angels to help him in need; Elisha had attending angels to help him when in need; and I believe we have attending angels to help us when we are in need.

What does this mean to us, practically speaking? Does the presence of angels mean they will always keep us from getting hurt? Sometimes. As with Elisha, our connection with the spiritual will warn us or protect us from harm. Praise God when that happens. But sometimes, as with Jesus and Paul and others, the decisions of sinful men will affect or hurt us in the natural world, but our connection with the spiritual will give us the strength and courage to go through our day of evil without fear, giving us the confidence and perspective to come out on the other side victorious.

We need to remember, however, that the realm of heaven responds to our prayers of faith. we fail to offer those prayers of faith, then the angels are not released to engage the enemy coming against us. I believe that many angels sent to aid us in our struggles against the enemy are bound from interfering because we never release them in faith and prayer to do the jobs they were sent here to do.

As you may have surmised by now, I had strong Christian parents and helpful Christian counselors who helped me learn how to take authority over the spiritual attacks I faced as a teenager. I learned the steps to overcome fear and how to take control of my thoughts and actions.

Of course, this was not an overnight cure, but a step in my journey to victory. From the beginning, there were nights of victory, where I confidently sent the man in black running out of the house. But there were other nights when I was not so strong and I allowed doubt creep into my thoughts. On one particular night, my parents heard me scream. As they came running into my room, they could feel the heaviness. I was lying on my bed, unresponsive, with a blank stare. They tried everything to pull me back to reality, but nothing worked. Mom picked up the phone in the middle of the night and called my counselor. "Pray," the counselor said. "If you don't get her back now, you may lose her forever." Mom and Dad spent the next few hours praying over me, and eventually it broke and I came back to reality.

I continued to learn to rebuke the evil spirit on my own; and as I grew more and more confident of my identity in Christ, the victories became bigger and the defeats smaller until the spirit of fear finally left. It tried to return a few times over the following year; but every time I practiced the things I had learned, it had to leave.

In the beginning, the battle was fierce, and it required constant prayer and alertness to keep the spirit of fear from winning. If I let my guard (the armor of God) down, the spirit of fear was there to control my thoughts in an instant, and the fear would almost hypnotize me and take me immediately into flashbacks. It was always the desire of this spirit to control me through fear and remind me of what had happened. It also continually reminded me of my most powerless moments, convincing me that my identity was defined by my weakest times.

But as I continued to put the spiritual disciplines I had learned into practice, they became more natural. As I grew stronger, the fear grew weaker. Then one day, realizing it could not longer beat me, the spirit of fear left me and the battle was over. I had taken my stand and resisted the devil and he had fled from me (James 4:7).

After this, I was able to get on with my life. I continued to be a cheerleader and a leader in our youth group, and I took a job in town—all the reasons that required me to stay in town late and drive home after dark.

I know that if I had not fought this battle, I would have become one of those people condemned to live with their phobia. Driving after dark would have been just one more item on the list of things I did not do. The enemy would have continued to keep score, tallying one more for the bad guys. When we do not face the spirit of fear head-on with the power of the Holy Spirit, Scripture, and truth, it grows bigger and stronger. It will eventually render you disabled in the spiritual realm and steal every shred of abundance and joy in your life. We have been given all power and all authority over the darkness in our lives (Mark 16:17-18; Luke 10:19). Unless we align ourselves with that power, the lights will stay out and the battle will be won over you.

As I grew in my understanding of the spiritual world and the spiritual resources around me, my faith grew, my confidence grew, and fear lost its hold on me. That is when I became a victor. It is our understanding of the spiritual realm that leads to our faith and authority.

Whatever reality is more real to you is the reality from which your responses will flow. Then your responses will determine which reality you invite to control the situation. You may say that you trust in God, but how do you respond in the moment of fear? Do you look at the natural world and feed the fear? Or do you choose to look into the spirit through prayer, through trusting what you have studied, and through listening to the Holy Spirit and gaining courage in what you hear? Your answer to this question will determine how your life progresses from this point forward.

Boldness in the power of the One who sent you is invaluable. It is imperative that you know not only who your God is but also who you are in him.

> Then Moses summoned Joshua and said to him in the presence of all Israel, "Be strong and courageous, for you must go with this people into the land that the Lord swore to their ancestors to give them, and you must divide it among them as their inheritance. The Lord himself goes before you and will be with you; he will never leave you nor forsake you. Do not be afraid; do not be discouraged." (Deut. 31:7–8)

Fear and hopelessness were some of my biggest giants until the time came when I learned these principles and put them into practice. Remember by whose power we fight and remember to see the giant through the eyes of the Father and not through the eyes of the Israelite army. How big is your God? David's God was bigger than anything that came against him. Following the leading of God in our lives will result in a life of peace, no matter what the world throws at you.

> "I have told you these things, so that in me you may have peace. In this world you will have trouble. But take heart! I have overcome the world." (John 16:33)

Overcoming fear was a life-changing paradigm shift for me. But overcoming fear is not just a discipline of the mind; it is a process of learning to see and understand the world from a different spiritual perspective. There are spiritual realities of our identity under God that not only overcome existing fear but that can also prevent fear from gaining a foothold in the first place. This is the spiritual understanding that brought boldness and power to King David and to the prophet Elisha.

Let's slay the giants in the land and take on our commission to set the captives free!

> The Spirit of the Sovereign Lord is on me, because the Lord has anointed me to proclaim good news to the poor. He has sent me to bind up the brokenhearted, to proclaim freedom for the captives and release from darkness for the prisoners, to proclaim the year of the Lord's favor and the day of vengeance of our God, to comfort all who mourn, and provide for those who grieve in Zion—to bestow on them a crown of beauty instead of ashes, the oil of joy instead of mourning, and a garment of praise instead of a spirit of despair. They will be called oaks of righteousness, a planting of the Lord for the display of his splendor. (Isa. 61:1–3)

Issues in Marriage

After high school, I planned to go to college. After one semester at a Christian college, though, I was frustrated and disillusioned. I had no focus or direction in school, and the spiritual atmosphere was not what I had expected. I came home for Christmas break; and when the short break was over, I reluctantly packed my car as the tears of disappointment and dissatisfaction began to flow. I remember sitting in the driveway talking to my mom. She knew full well that the tears were not all homesick tears.

She said, "You know you don't have to go back, right?"

The words hit me like a Mack truck. The tears erupted into a full-blown meltdown, and I got out of the car, went in the house, and sat on the couch. That was the end of college.

So, what now? Feeling as though I had no direction and had failed at the one grown-up thing I had tried, I cried myself to sleep that night, relieved not to be going back to college but at a loss as to what was next. Through the years before college, the only real directional constant I had was my call to ministry and to missions. Although I had attempted to pursue this through Bible college, it was not a fit. So I decided to pursue both missions and biblical training together by exploring a missions-based discipleship training course. This was the only move that felt right, but it would be the first time I ventured out into missions on my own, without Mom and Dad. I was both nervous and excited.

I landed a job the next week, and within the month I pursued a plan to join the Youth ith a Mission (YWAM) Discipleship Training School (DTS) that was held on board the Mercy Ship *Anastasis.* By August

1994 I had saved up my tuition money and I was nineteen years old and off to begin DTS. Day one: Fly from Seattle to Dallas. Day two: Meet my future husband, David. Mind you, I did not know that at the time!

So began my journey into the future and my quest to know God in a deeper way. David and I walked that road together. He was all I could ask for in a friend, and since we were not allowed to date during the training, we had the opportunity to focus on building a lasting friendship built on our relationship with God.

The first half of our DTS was the training phase where we spent 8-10 hours a day in bible study, prayer, and spiritual growth lectures. The DTS started in Lindale, Texas, which is just outside of Tyler; but we were there only for a few months before we flew to the Netherlands where the Mercy Ship Anastasis was ending a time in drydock. We boarded the ship in Holland and spent a few weeks helping get her ready to sail.

I worked in the purser's office getting passports and other paperwork in order. David worked on the repair crew that spent their time patching holes, fixing pipes, removing rust, painting, and anything else that needed to be done. In the evenings many of us would walk the twenty minutes from the docks into the small town of Perth to hang out at the one local coffee shop/pub.

It was a great time of growing closer to God, building new friendships, and feeling like we were helping to make a difference in the ministry of the Mercy Ships. One weekend we took a trip with fiev or six other students to Antwerp, Belgium where we stayed in a youth hostile and explored the city. Every time we went into town or took a weekend trip there were different people in the crowd. But the one constant was me and David – walking together, talking, laughing, and I felt safe because I knew he was always watching out for me.

After clearing drydock, we sailed for Cardiff, Wales where we took on more crew and supplies that would be needed during the six-month medical outreach the team would be doing in various ports in Africa. Most of our days were still spent in studies, lectures, prayer, and doing our work duties. However, in the evenings and on weekends we had time to explore Cardiff. It was a fun town with nice parks, fish and chips restaurants, and some quaint little pubs with game rooms.

Once all the crew and supplies were onboard, we set sail for the Canary Islands where the ship would take on fuel and let us off. The second half of every YWAM DTS is the outreach phase where the entire school goes somewhere in the world to do three months of outreach based on everything they have learned in the teaching phase. Our outreach was in the Canary Islands.

We set up home for the next three months in a small campground on the island of Tenerife. The campground consisted of about thirty little green 'houses' that were really just ten-by-ten rooms big enough for four bunks. There was a central kitchen and meeting room where we ate, planned our outreaches, relaxed, and played cards. For me, this was home for the next three months. There was a tourist beach and shopping center about a 10-minute drive from our campground where we would do our outreaches. But in time, our DTS came to an end. David felt called to stay in the Canary Islands and possibly work smuggling Bibles into Mauritania. Although the Bible smuggling never panned out, he did stay in the Canaries for two years doing ministry with a local church in the city of Las Palmas on the island of Grand Canary. At this point, I felt I was called to be a pastor's wife, so I reasoned that he was not the one for me. We said our good-byes, and I returned home.

Lies of Inadequacy

After my DTS I returned home and became involved leading one of the local youth groups. Eventually, I got engaged to the one of the other leaders. He was charismatic and outgoing, and we seemed to share a call for ministry and a love for youth. Although he did not treat me like my dad treated my mom, it was good enough, I thought. I was blind to the dynamics that were really going on between us. He convinced me of many things that were not true about myself. He saw the boundaries I had set up in regard to watching movies that contained violence and abuse, and my needing lights on, as weakness. Whether he intended to or not, he continually communicated to me that I was broken and unworthy. He never took the time or interest to understand what I had been through and how far I had come. His expectations of me were to be "normal" by his standards. The unconscious effect of this on me was profound.

His expectations and the lies he communicated sent me back to a place of agreement with the enemy that my identity was found in my weakest moment, and I began to act defeated in every aspect of my life. I lost all the strength I had gained in knowing who I was. I allowed my fiancé to treat me disrespectfully, and I began to live out those traits he believed to be true about me. My parents became concerned and tried on several occasions to remind me of the truth. But my eyes were blinded, as I accepted the false truth that I was broken and not worthy of anything better. All my decisions at this time were made from that foundation.

This was yet another attempt of the enemy to render me ineffective in the kingdom of God. Yet the hand of the Lord was working in my life in a way I did not see or understand. Three weeks before the wedding, my fiancé had an affair with one of my best friends, and all of the lies that held up the facade of our relationship began to crumble. The Spirit of truth was at work, exposing the darkness for what it was.

But now, at twenty years old, I was once again lost, alone, and betrayed. My mom quit her job and poured her energy into spending time with me. We passed the mornings walking around the lake, and we prayed and talked quite a bit. She prayed over me and for me. She read the Bible to me and was the healing balm I needed. Through her love and support, although I experienced heartbreak and sadness, I was not depressed.

I remember telling Mom on one of those walks that I felt like I was in a tornado and the world was swirling all around me but that I was being held in the eye of the storm, a place that was safe and quiet. All the while, she taught me how to walk through this different kind of trauma. She helped me to fix my eyes on Jesus and allow the truth of his love to restore me and set me free again. She modeled for me the true meaning of joy in spite of my circumstances.

Accepting Positive Voices in our Lives

One day around that time, my dad and I went four-wheeling up the side of a mountain. During the course of the ride, he asked me what I wanted. I told him I wanted someone who would treat me like David had during our YWAM DTS. When we returned home, we continued the conversation. Then he asked me if I trusted him.

"Sure," I told him.

At that, Dad picked up the phone and called the Canary Islands where David was still serving as a missionary. When he got David on the phone, the conversation was short. "Hello David," my father began. "This is Darrell Beebe."

"Hello," David responded. "What can I do for you?"

Dad didn't waste any time. "How's your love life?"

"Well, I'm in a Spanish-speaking country and I don't speak Spanish very well. So it's not that great," David quipped back. "Why?"

As I about hit the floor, Dad asked, "You still got anything left in your heart for my daughter?"

"Yes," was his simple reply, and again, David asked, "Why?"

"Good, here she is," Dad finished and handed me the phone.

I was nearly speechless but managed to say something, although I don't really remember what. I do know that I shared how my engagement had fallen through. We talked for a while, and then we began e-mailing back and forth for a few months.

In time, we met in England, where David's sister and brother-in-law were living. After a week together, we were engaged. Six months later we were married.

The first year was great. We had all the adventures of a young couple just starting out. But after a while some things from my past began to creep into our relationship, dark things that challenged our unity and our joy.

Sometimes we do not understand the effects that previous hurts and offenses can have on our future relationships. For us, there were a number of hurdles we had to overcome in the first few years of marriage. You, too, may find that the past is challenging your present in ways that are detrimental to you. But take heart—there is a way through. God is a God of restoration!

First were the emotional issues. After I married David, without being aware of it, I began to transfer my perception of previous romantic relationships and what others may have believed about me onto David. I read what he said and did through this subconscious filter of my unresolved and unhealed woundedness. This caused walls between us, because I felt the need to protect myself. The barriers I put up were rooted in feelings I could not consciously understand or define. David would say or do something that triggered a response in me from a memory of my past relationship, and it all happened so fast and subconsciously, I did not recognize what was going on: I was allowing old hurt to define my new relationship.

After a while, we began to have a number of talks where David had to remind me, "I am not your former boyfriend; stop reacting like I am." It took time and affirmation—and a great deal of patience on his part. But the healing eventually came, and I began to see David for who he was. Confidence came with that.

I had married my best friend and the love of my life. David truly was and is my knight in shining armor. He loves me beyond comprehension, and he is without a doubt God's best and abundant plan for my life.

Sexual Problems

Beyond that, though, there were also sexual issues to be resolved. On the first night of our honeymoon, the bliss of true love was interrupted with the reality of my past abuse. The dream gave way to reality when it was time to disrobe on that first night. I was consumed by fear and insecurity. I couldn't go through with this physical intimacy.

Feeling like a failure as a wife, I called home in tears. David was patient and understanding. He told me that a physical relationship was not the reason he had married me and that we would work this out in time. But after we had our first few days and nights together, I was able to relax and be intimate. None-the-less, this experience made me realized I still had some hills to climb.

Climbing these hills was made harder by my lack of transparency with David about what I had been through. I did not want to be regarded as weak again, as I had been in my previous relationship, so I changed the story I told David about my past. I wanted him to see me as strong and not as a victim, so the story he heard was that our family was attacked on the mission field and we were over it. As a family, we made jokes about it and made light of it in front of him. For the first few years into our marriage, he really did not have a clue as to the extent of what I had been through because we had watered it down. I felt the need to be strong and to "handle" whatever came up. This allowed one more of those walls to wedge itself into the middle of our physical relationship. Because what David did not know was that half of the time when we were being intimate, something would happen that would trigger a flashback and I would be fighting it the whole time.

When they happened, I felt like I couldn't tell David. I was still holding on to being strong and not giving in. I did not want to show any weakness to him. I did not want to be broken. I did not want to be a disappointment. I was afraid of what that might mean in my marriage. I refused to be limited or defined by my past, but at that point, I was also refusing to truly deal with it out of fear of reliving that pain.

Because I did not know how to fix the problem, however, I suffered in silence. This caused struggles not only in our physical relationship but also in my ability to receive love from David. I was allowing my feelings of fear and the flashbacks once again to cloud my vision about who he really was, that he truly loved me, and that we could work it out together.

Sexual Empowerment

Because he was sensitive to the Holy Spirit, David knew there was something wrong; but he didn't know what it was, let alone how to fix it. He did realize that the overall problems we were having in our marriage had to do with us being physically intimate and that we needed to talk about it. He told me that we could forego that part of our relationship indefinitely if that was what I needed.

David's ability to be so selfless began to tear down the lies I believed about what I needed to "endure" to be a good wife. The safety this created for me gave me the strength to finally open up to him and tell him the whole story. So one night we stayed up all night. We sat in front of the fireplace downstairs, and I shared with him all the details of the story of Palau that I had withheld from him. Although it was uncomfortable, it was also freeing. That honesty gave him a new understanding and gave us both a foundation for restarting this part of our relationship. This was three years into our marriage.

It took a lot of honesty and patience on both sides to get through this time. We finally came to the understanding that part of the flashbacks had to do with smells and touches. Those were easy enough to avoid once defined. But there was another aspect of the flashbacks that had to do with helplessness. The night in Palau I had felt helpless, without any control of the situation. Without realizing it, I had come to associate sex with that loss of control. Anytime David and I were intimate, I felt that he was in control and I had to do whatever he wanted or else I was a bad wife. I felt no control, no power to say "stop" if something hurt or caused a flashback feeling.

The solution for us was to empower me with control in this part of our relationship. If something hurt, I could say "stop." If I was not in the mood, I could say so. If I needed something from him, I could ask for it. For some of you this may be elementary, but for someone who has been abused this is a great revelation.

We agreed to a time of abstaining from our physical relationship, allowing the Holy Spirit to teach us how to navigate this part of our marriage. This lasted about a month or two. David's continued love and tenderness finally melted the walls of "safety" I had put up. At long last, I was able to see his real heart, his real love, for me went far beyond just sex. After three years of marriage, I was truly able to trust him to truly love me.

Although the biggest part of this healing happened quickly, it took the next few years for us to really work out this part of my healing. What it produced was a strong and healthy sexual relationship that we both enjoy, and it healed the woundedness that my silence had created.

We worked together on the same side, and my husband was no longer the enemy, the one causing me pain or fear. Once again, the principle of the confession of the truth brought freedom from the prison of secrecy.

After counseling numerous couples over the years and leading several conferences on marriage, we have found that problems with physical intimacy are an area of secrecy for many women. Some suffer in silence for five, ten, twenty, or more years without telling their spouses what they are dealing with. As a result, sex becomes a point of pain for one partner and a source of animosity for the other. This leaves neither happy nor fulfilled in this area of marriage, which God created to be one of the most intimate connections between a man and woman. Being honest with each other about your past and empowering each other in this area is vital to developing a strong and healthy sexual relationship.

After David and I worked through these sexual issues, my nightmares and flashbacks finally ended. I was whole, healed, and in control of my life. I had dealt with everything from my past, and I had found victory in all the areas that once held me down.

For many, this is the end of the road. But God had one more stop for me on my journey. In 2007, I would come face-to-face again with one of the men who had raped me. The feelings that came over me in that moment were nothing I could have expected, and nothing short of amazing.

Return to Palau

In 2006, David finished his initial commitment with the army; and after praying, we felt it was time to move on. David took a position as the senior pastor of a small-town church in Indiana. So we packed up our home in Georgia and started the move across country. We were not set to start at the new church until the first of the year, so we took our time traveling across the country. The older boys were six and seven years old and Isaac was just about six months so we were not planning on much cross-country travel after we got settled in Indiana. So we took advantage of this time to stop at a number of tourist stops along the way like Washington D.C. and Hershey Park. We spent a few weeks with family in South Carolina and in Virginia Beach along the way because we didn't know how long it would be before we saw them again.

There were not many commitments and our schedule was empty, so we had a lot of time for family and for personal reading and prayer time. One morning I was sitting on the porch at David's sister's house in South Carolina overlooking the creek and lake, having my quiet time. After a while, I called my mom to talk, and she dropped some surprising news on me: The family had been invited to return to Palau for a two-week mission and celebration trip. We would be preaching in various churches, meeting with island leaders, and holding one large outdoor crusade. For my parents, this was the final chapter, a chance to close the book and come full circle. They were excited to see God's hand of blessing, and it was a chance for us all to minister healing and forgiveness to the people of Palau. We had received a message from the local pastors through the local missionary that the people of Palau would hear differently from us than they might from anyone else.

I, however, was not so excited. An unexpected feeling of uneasiness came over me. They could go if they wanted to, but not me. I was free. I was healed. I had nothing left to face. The more I kept telling myself this, the more I began to realize it wasn't true. There was something still there that I needed to put to rest. I didn't know what it was; but as much as I hated to face the facts, I knew I had to go.

How quickly the spirit of fear can sneak up on you. It is also alarming to me how it can mask itself as so many other things, such as concern or logic, so that you do not recognize it quickly enough to deal with it. Just a few seconds is all that spirit needs to take root. Once it has taken root, the work is done and we are the ones who water it. It grows and spreads before we can catch our breath.

So many thoughts ran through my head. *What makes them think I am stupid enough to go back there? Why would my family go and risk their lives again? Don't they know what that will do to me? I will be worried sick the whole time they are gone! Surely God would not ask us to do something like this a second time. Haven't we done enough?*

It is amazing what we can convince ourselves about God's will when our perspective stems from the realm of fear.

So, fear took over, disguised as logic and concern. By simply not recognizing and resisting this tactic of the enemy, I opened up a previously closed door for that spirit to come and affect me once again. I spent the next week battling nightmares and anxiety and anger. This kept me agitated and frustrated. I had no desire to press in to the presence of God. I was unable to find refuge in him.

Sometimes when we are oppressed by the enemy, we remain locked up emotionally and spiritually. We tend to avoid that place of breakthrough in the Holy Spirit, because we lose the drive to fight through to him. At these times we must, like David in the Psalms, push though our feelings and press in anyway, knowing that God will meet us on the other side.

The worst part for me was that the trip was scheduled for the spring of 2007, less than six months into our new pastorate. This meant that David would not be able to go with me. He would have to stay behind and take care of the kids and the church. I was not happy about this, but I knew that God was calling me to go. None-the-less, I needed to pray through it.

Anger and desperation drove me to that quiet place alone with my God, and this is how the conversation went.

Me: "I can't believe you would ask me to do this. Haven't I done everything you have asked me to do? Haven't I been faithful to climb every mountain erected in front of me? Is this your opportunity to show me how weak I am when I thought I had come so far? Why would you ask me to revisit the dark places I have come from, now, when I have children to take care of and a life to live? I haven't slept in days; I'm tormented by nightmares. Why would you put my family at risk like this?"

God's voice came back clear: "Do you want to know why I am sending you back, or are you going to keep throwing a fit? You have allowed the spirit of fear to convince you that I have evil in store for you. Don't you know it is my plan to take you to a place of ultimate blessing? It is my desire to bless you beyond your wildest dreams and to show you how far you have come, not to take you back to a place of pain. Child, you have been faithful in your healing, and now it is time to celebrate and rejoice. Go to Palau and receive all I have waiting for you there!"

I knew that it was God's will for me to return to Palau with my family. The enemy knew this and twisted the truth just enough to get me angry with God, to keep me from seeking clarity on this issue. What the enemy said was, "You still have some healing to do [which was true], so you need to return to Palau to face the giants of your past to complete your healing [false]." The truth was that God desired to bless me abundantly, to reward me, to show me how far I had come, and to allow me to see the fruit of my labor.

It was only because I knew the heart of my loving Father that I was able to see the lie of the enemy, which told me that God wanted me to trudge through old battles long since laid to rest and go back to a place of ultimate pain and defeat. Eventually, I understood that the truth was that God's desire was to prosper me and not to harm me, to bring hope and a future (Jer. 29:11).God spoke to me one day and gave me a Scripture that showed me what he had in store for us in Palau:

> As they pass through the Valley of Baka, they make it a place of springs; the autumn rains also cover it with pools. They go from strength to strength, till each appears before God in Zion.
> (Ps. 84:6–7)

The Valley of Baka is commonly understood to mean the valley of weeping. While there are different reasons for this interpretation, most commentators interpret these verses to signify that as we go through places that have brought or would otherwise bring us to tears (fear, sadness, pain), if we focus on and follow God's leading, he will bring refreshing, life-giving "rain" to us instead. By this, instead of being overcome by the enemy, we will instead grow in the strength of the Lord. The very thing that by earthly appearance should bring us fear and sadness, in the spiritual will bring us strength and joy. Once I heard God speak this to me, I became very excited. From that point on, my perspective on the trip changed and I joyfully began making plans to return to Palau.

When the day finally came to leave for Palau, I said my good-byes to David and the kids, wishing they were going with me but also relieved that with what I was facing, I would only be taking care of me. I traveled to Seattle where I joined the rest of the group that was going. My parents, my brother and I, of course, were all going. We were also accompanied by my sister-in-law, my parent's best friends, and a photographer that the Assemblies of God was sending to document the trip for an article they planned to write in the Pentecostal Evangel, the Assemblies of God magazine that had first published our story many years before.

The trip was long, but I was among friends and family and enjoyed the reunion. As we left Guam (our first stop) and headed for Palau, we all had our moments of withdrawing into silence to process what was coming. There was no turning back now. Whatever we hoped for, expected, or thought might happen, it was all about to shortly unfold for us.

Many Surprises

Almost two hours after taking off from Guam, we began our descent into Palau. Although it was evening, I could still make out the rock islands scattered across this western portion of the Pacific Ocean.

Palau International Airport is located on the little island of Koror, where the Palau's main city is located. As we banked left to line up with the runway, we could see the bridge linking Koror to the big island of Babelthuap. The lights of the small city of Koror glimmered across the water and we could see a few headlights crossing the bridge. On Babelthuap, there was not much to be seen in the dark of the approaching night.

We landed and taxied to a new airport terminal, which had been built in recent years. We gathered our belongings and made our way off the plane and down to baggage. After going through customs, we headed down the hallway that led to the main lobby of the terminal, where someone would hopefully be there to meet us with our name on a cardboard sign.

As we came around the corner, I was shocked at the large gathering of people. There must have been fifty to seventy people. I wondered who they were there for until I read the large banner over their heads that said, *Welcome Beebe Family.* Then many of these people began hugging us and showering us with flower leis, singing, "What a Mighty God We Serve." I felt so honored and loved, and I was moved beyond words or tears.

As we got in the van that would take us to the hotel, we were all speechless and a mess of emotions, thanking God for this blessing and for whatever he had in store for us. That was the first point at which I realized that I would likely be far more blessed by this trip than I would bless others.

The next morning, we headed to church. The building was simple by American standards but it was amazing to us compared to the chicken coop we had met in more than twenty years prior! As I took in the music and looked around at the hundred-plus Palauans worshiping God, my heart was overwhelmed once again. We had started something two decades earlier that the enemy tried to snuff out, and the Holy Spirit had breathed life into it. It was now a strong and thriving church.

At the end of the service, we had a surprise visit from the governor of the Palauan state of Airai. She asked to speak and as she did, with head downcast, she asked on behalf of the state of Airai for our forgiveness. She then said that the state was shamed by what those men did to us; and if we would forgive them, then maybe God would bless the nation again. As far as I knew, she was not a follower of Christ, but she certainly understood the power and the principles of forgiveness. It was our joy to extend the forgiveness that we had already experienced in our hearts to the nation through her. We also took that opportunity to let the people know we had come back not to shame the nation but to bring a message of God's hope, healing, and forgiveness. Once again, we were completely overwhelmed, not only by God's plan to bless us in this country but by the honor we received from the people.

In our planning for this trip, God had put it on our hearts to offer a banquet to honor the heads of state. Invitations went out, and we planned to host the dinner at the hotel where we were staying. We learned just before the event, however, that the president of Palau was also hosting a formal event the same night. Not sure what to expect, we were happily surprised to receive a large turnout. We then took the evening to honor those present and share with them God's love for their country and their people. We also had the opportunity to honor those who had volunteered for the search committee to find my mom years ago and to meet them face-to-face once again.

As the evening came to a close, the vice president of the nation asked to address the crowd. We were shocked once again as he asked for our forgiveness. The leaders also expressed their intention to implement into their government what they had learned that evening about forgiveness. A great healing began for the country that night. We were later told that there had recently been much unrest in the government and that some had been planning to overthrow the current leadership. But with a new understanding of forgiveness and hope, those plans dissolved.

God did so many things each day to honor and uplift us. Although we had come to serve, we were completely surprised time and time again as the Palauan people overwhelmed us with honor and love.

The day after the gathering with these government leaders, we spent an amazing day on the water, as some of the local church members had arranged a picnic for us on a beautiful uninhabited island, followed by a boat tour of the rock islands as well as some of the most incredible snorkeling in the world. We hiked to a lake in the middle of a rock island called Jellyfish Lake where there were millions of jellyfish. Fortunately for us they were the kind that do not sting! We swam around the lake and enjoyed the magnificent beauty of the islands.

Facing the Past

On another afternoon we decided to make the drive out to our old house. I didn't decide to go until the last minute. I was going to pass and then decided I was not going to let fear make any decisions for me on this trip.

As we drove down the bumpy road, we all grew silent as we neared the house. The house was impossible to miss. It was dark and run-down but looked just as I remembered. I sat for several long moments before leaving the safety of the van. As I sat there, I struggled to separate the pictures in my head from the reality of where I was now. The dark, violent terror of that night twenty years earlier collided with this peaceful and serene day. My eyes locked onto the places where I had been abused.

The images were so clear and so real, I had to ask the Holy Spirit to give me peace and strength to see his deliverance and protection.

As I stepped out of the van, indeed I felt his strength and the bad memories slowly transformed to the milestones and victories God had led me to in the years since. I thanked him for where I was now, for delivering my family, and for bringing us back to this place to glorify him. The enemy was completely defeated in our lives, and God had restored our hearts and our hope. Tears of sorrow mixed with tears of joy in knowing true victory, as we all embraced and prayed together in that place. We thanked God for his perfect plan and for his protection, provision, and blessings for our family.

The next day was Wednesday, and it arrived with great anticipation. This is when we would begin the outdoor revival meetings we had long since planned. Each of us would share what God had given us to say to the people of Palau.

It was so exciting to see the people fill the stands. As we mingled with the crowd, I could not help but remember something I had felt the Holy Spirit tell me as I was getting ready that night. He had told me that I was going to see one of the men who attacked us. I had quickly responded, "Not my will but yours, God." The thought brought a shudder, but just as swiftly I was comforted by the countless times we had been surprised by God that week. I knew I could trust him.

I was walking through the stands with my dad when someone stopped him and pointed to a man sitting alone with his head down. Dad whispered to me to go back to the field while he talked to this man. I knew immediately who he was. I also knew this was a moment in time I would never get back. I turned to my dad and said, "I want to do this." In the next moment, my mom and brother were with us, and together the four of us approached the man who had spent twenty years in a dark prison cell for what he had done to our family.

Dad was the first to speak. Kneeling in front of the man, who was still looking down at the ground, he took his hand and shared forgiveness from his heart. When I looked the man in the eyes, I felt sorry for him. He was so broken, an empty shell. This man who haunted my dreams could not even look me in the eye. I had no anger or hate toward him. I only felt sorry for him. I knew that Satan had intended to use him to destroy us, and then he had turned and destroyed him.

I cannot tell you what it did for me to be able to look into the eyes of a man who was instrumental in bringing so much destruction and so much fear and feel nothing but pity and mercy. We had the opportunity to be Jesus to him. At that moment, God brought to my mind the passage:

> For our struggle is not against flesh and blood but against the rulers, against the authorities, against the powers of this dark world and against the spiritual forces of evil in the heavenly realms. (Eph. 6:12)

I told the man that I forgave him and that I wanted him to experience the same healing we had. I told him that God loved him and wanted to heal his heart. As we walked away, I deeply felt God's heart of compassion for his people. I also felt a bit like David when he released that small smooth stone into the head of his giant.

God does not require everyone to eventually face their abusers. There is often no point in doing so. And I do not believe our return to Palau was for this purpose. I believe he sent us back to Palau for the sake of many who would come to faith or find healing through our story. However, God often accomplishes multiple things in one event. For me, he allowed me to see the blessings he had brought to a nation through our pain. He allowed me to look at someone who had caused me much fear for years and see him from a completely different perspective, both in the natural and the spiritual He allowed me to extend personal forgiveness to the man I had forgiven before God years ago. These are blessings not many get to experience, and I am grateful for them.

The power of healing and hope supercharged the rest of the meeting that night, and God did many amazing physical miracles for and through the Palauan people. Nothing has so impacted my life as that opportunity to open the door for many to experience God's forgiveness and to understand the freedom of extending forgiveness.

One of the last excursions planned for us in Palau was a visit to a waterfall. Now doesn't that sound refreshing and peaceful? At this point, I was in the first few months of my fourth pregnancy. The "short walk" down to the waterfall turned out to be quite an adventure. The journey took approximately an hour and included the need for a walking stick, climbing with all fours, and traversing a river. Most of the trail was in the path of a river, which was slippery and rocky. All the way in, I was fully aware that this steep mountain we were sliding down now would be much more of a challenge on the way out.

When we finally arrived, it was worth the effort. The waterfall was breathtaking. It came seemingly out of nowhere and plunged into a beautiful and serene pool. We swam to the center of the pool and climbed up on a large rock. As a family, we began to pray and to praise God for the victory this place represented in our lives. The Spirit of God fell, and his presence was heavy as the blessings came down. The Holy Spirit reminded me of the Scripture he had given me in preparation for the trip:

> As they pass through the Valley of Baka [weeping], they make it a place of springs; the autumn rains also cover it with pools. They go from strength to strength, till each appears before God in Zion.
> (Ps. 84:6–7)

I was incredibly aware of the connection between the spiritual journey I had taken to get to this place of healing and the journey I had taken in the natural world to see this amazing waterfall God had created. It is remarkable to me that God never does one thing at a time. He had raised up an entire generation since we were last in Palau, a generation of people who know his name, who are changing the spiritual tide and rewriting history for Palau.

The reality was that we didn't go back to Palau to face our fears. We went back to claim the inheritance that God had promised us. And that inheritance was good.

The Day of Evil

In his Letter to the Ephesians, Paul talks about what to do when the day of evil comes. It is interesting that he does not say "if" your day of evil comes. He says "when" your day of evil comes; it is assumed that we will face days of evil in this life. Jesus also warned us that we would suffer trials of many kinds because we follow him, and Paul here tells us how to prepare:

Therefore put on the full armor of God, so that when the day of evil comes, you may be able to stand your ground, and after you have done everything, to stand. (Eph. 6:13)

The concept of the day of evil or suffering is something we seem to have left out of the description of the Christian life. Maybe that's because it works better for evangelistic purposes to not mention it. The abundant life of Christianity is much more enticing! I am a solid believer in the abundant life and will talk about it later in this book. I believe, however, that the balance of these two concepts needs to be better understood.

The abundant life comes from a mature and godly perspective on your life that develops when you are able to understand your identity and authority in Christ in the spiritual realm. We live in two realms: one spiritual and one physical. Whichever realm is more real to you is the realm in which you will live the majority of the time, and it is the realm that will have the most effect on your emotional life. The heavenly realm existed before the creation of the world and will exist for eternity, long after this world passes away. One realm directly affects the other. If you can walk in obedience to God and experience the power of the heavenly realm through the guidance of the Holy Spirit in your life, then you will have authority over the physical world around you and over the forces of darkness that try to afflict you. If, however, you give in to the enemy's temptations to walk in worldly emotions of anger, fear, and pride, then these emotions will control your outlook and block your ability to enter into the peace of God and the authority of his kingdom.

Until you reach the point where you are able to understand and experience the concept that you have "all authority on heaven and earth," you will experience days of evil in different ways. You may not experience the same day of evil that I did, but the truth is that this world is under the influence of the devil until the final judgment comes. He has the ability to throw fiery darts at you, and they will continue to hurt until you are able to see the world through spiritual eyes and know your place in the kingdom.

This does not mean that you will never experience evil in life (although I do believe you will experience less, because you will be less likely to walk into it blindly). But it means that when days of evil do come, you will be able to stand against them in a different way. In some cases, you will have the power and authority to physically divert them. In other cases, you may suffer evil in the natural world, but your spirit will stand strong and will weather through the storm. The stones of humans may hurt your body, but the flaming spiritual darts of the enemy that accompany those stones will not penetrate your spiritual armor.

God Gets a Bad Rap

God often unfairly gets the blame for our day of evil. When bad things happen to people, they often blame God for not preventing this. There are theological perspectives that God will even send days of evil upon us in order to teach us a lesson. We call this the "mysterious ways of God." While it is true that God will allow us to be tested for our growth, he does not send evil upon us. He tests us for our good and to bring the best out in us. He does not send calamity upon us.

The truth is that evil comes upon us for different reasons. One is that we live in a fallen world, and God has granted free will to humanity. Other people, under their own bad choices and as they are tempted by the enemy, may choose to bring us harm. Jesus clearly warned us to expect tribulation in this world (John 16:33). Jesus even said that as Christians we can expect more of it than non-Christians, because we are standing for him in a world that hates him (John 15:18–21). We are in a battle zone, and there will be casualties. Days of evil will come on everyone.

But even in this we should take joy, because we know he has overcome the world. If we remain in him, he will bring us through and we will experience spiritual joy and blessing in the process. The problem is that when some people experience evil, they immediately become angry with God and cut off contact with Jesus, thus cutting their only lifeline.

Another way that evil comes upon us is when we make our own bad choices and have to suffer the consequences of those choices. In Romans 8, Paul tells us that if we remain constantly connected to the Holy Spirit and allow him to lead us, then the evils of this world will not rule over us. Not many people, however, allow the Spirit to lead them on a daily basis, and they do not listen to his guidance in every decision. As a result, they make the wrong choices at times. Sometimes they do hear the leading of the Spirit, but they choose to ignore it. The irony is that when the natural consequences of their own choices fall upon them, they still blame God and get angry with him for not protecting them. Hence, God gets a bad rap.

If the expectation of hard times is so clear through the teachings of Christ and Paul, then why do so many Christians expect a perfect, carefree life? Why do they get angry at God when bad things happen? He not only warned us about this happening, but he has given us the tools and the weapons to not only survive the days of evil but also to fight back and be victorious in them! Perspective is vital in this process.

God can win with any hand. Since he knows the future, he knows what things in our life can bring great blessing and what things he can use to prosper us the most. When the day of evil comes, the devil brings different tactics to try to destroy us and our relationship with God. First, he tries to get us to blame God for his evil work in our life. Then, if he cannot get us to turn our bitterness toward God, then he will try to focus it on ourselves or on others.

To help clarify this, I want to share with you a word my dad received one day while sitting on the platform preparing to preach at the prison in Palau. Between the time of worship and the message, twelve inmates accepted Jesus as their Lord and Savior. It was in this context that Dad heard an audible word: "Darrell, do you want to know why people suffer?" When Dad asked why, this is what he heard:

> *When my Son came into the world, I was concerned about his physical comfort and safety, and what men did to him broke my heart. But I was less concerned with his physical comfort and safety than I was with the spiritual condition of a lost and dying world. What happened to you and your family in Palau was of great concern to me, and what men did to you broke my heart, but I was less concerned with your physical comfort and safety than I was with the spiritual condition of this lost and dying nation. Had I not withheld my hand of protection twenty-one years ago, the names of these twelve men would not be in the Lamb's Book of Life tonight. When your family's comfort and safety was on one side of the scales of time and the souls of these twelve men were on the other side, I withheld my hand and the scale tipped in their favor. But remember, son, when your soul and the souls of your family were on one side of the scales of time and my Son's comfort and safety was on the other side, I withheld my hand and the scale tipped in your favor.*

In the New Testament, we read about those who followed Jesus and how they suffered flogging, stoning, shipwrecks, imprisonment, abandonment, and rejection, just to name a few of their "abundant life" experiences.

I do not say this to arouse anxiety or a doomsday perspective on life for those who serve Christ, but to bring the reality of what Jesus said about life so that we have a proper expectation and a sober response. Do not let the enemy plant seeds of fear in you while I attempt to teach through this concept. Jesus was straightforward and honest when he told the disciples that there would be many spiritual blessings and physical provisions in following him, but that there would also be rejection by many.

It is my desire, as I try to bridge the gap between "the day of evil" and "the abundant life," to give you hope and a proper perspective for victory rather than aid the enemy in instilling fear over what he can bring.

When you see life through the spiritual realm rather than the physical realm, then the absolute truth of your spiritual stature and strength will be exposed. You alone have the choice to determine what type of a soldier you will be. A general is not made overnight, and a private will never lead the army into war.

Whose Report Will You Believe?

As we saw earlier regarding the Israelite excursion into Canaan, one central question to ask on the journey to forgiveness and recovery is, "Whose report will you believe?" One of the principal tools of the enemy is a lie planted at just the right time. Many Christian counselors attest that many of their clients are still bound, years later, with many physical, mental, and spiritual problems because of a root lie they believed about themselves, about God, or about a situation long ago. One of the most important keys on the road to recovery is to keep the enemy from being able to plant those lies; we do this by focusing purposefully and prayerfully on the truth of God.

In most everything in our lives that can serve to either set us back or propel us forward, there are two reports, two perspectives that fight for control of our minds. One comes from the Father; the other comes from the enemy.

Again, as we saw earlier, following the Exodus from Egypt, Moses sent twelve spies to explore the land of Canaan. While Joshua and Caleb believed in the Lord and reported the greatness of the land, the other ten were fearful and spread a bad report among the people.

> Then Caleb silenced the people before Moses and said, "We should go up and take possession of the land, for we can certainly do it."
> But the men who had gone up with him said, "We can't attack those people; they are stronger than we are." And they spread among the Israelites a bad report about the land they had explored. They said, "The land we explored devours those living in it. All the people we saw there are of great size. We saw the Nephilim there (the descendants of Anak come from the Nephilim). We seemed like grasshoppers in our own eyes, and we looked the same to them." (Num. 13:30-33)

> God then responded to Moses, "How long will this people treat me with contempt? How long will they refuse to believe in me, in spite of all the signs I have performed among them?" (Num. 14:11).

As a result of their believing the bad report, the Israelites' trek into the Promised Land stalled, and they wandered in the desert for forty years. Only Caleb and Joshua survived and finally tasted the fruit of their belief in God.

In the same way, believing the bad report of the enemy cause us to walk in a spiritual wilderness of darkness, depression, and despair. We must be on our guard not to fall into this trap. If we choose to believe the enemy, then we block God's word and work in our lives.

Another version of a false report is a false truth. In the book of Judges, the people of Israel were conquered over and over because they failed to see God's truth in their lives, choosing instead to walk in evil and do what was right in their own eyes. "In their own eyes" is another trap the devil uses in our day of evil to destroy us. We see the situation from a worldly perspective or from our own perspective alone, and then the enemy whispers a "truth" of the situation into our minds: "Look, God has abandoned you," or "It was your fault."

John the Baptist knew Jesus was the Christ, but when his own eyes did not see what he had expected and he found himself in prison, he fell into doubt. The enemy whispered uncertainty in his mind, causing him to think that perhaps he was mistaken. So he sent a messenger to ask Jesus if he really was the one. Jesus responded with a truth of the spiritual dimension of reality:

"Go back and report to John what you have seen and heard: The blind receive sight, the lame walk, those who have leprosy are cleansed, the deaf hear, the dead are raised, and the good news is proclaimed to the poor." (Luke 7:22)

God's voice is always there to counter the voice of the enemy, and it is our choice whose voice we listen to and believe.

Peter knew Jesus and walked with him. Yet when Jesus began to talk openly with the disciples about his death, Peter became confused. The world was not working the way he expected it should. God was not working in this ministry the way he thought he should. The truth he expected from his faith was not what was playing out in front of him. So he contested Jesus' plan, and Jesus rebuked him as being deceived by the lying "truth" of the enemy. Peter was looking at the situation from his religious, physical reality. But Jesus had to redirect him to the truth of God in the moment.

After Jesus' death, the disciples then believed the "truth" that Jesus was dead and that he must not have really been the Messiah. This was after Jesus had plainly told them multiple times that he would be betrayed, tried, killed, and then raised from the dead. Jesus had plainly told them this spiritual truth, yet these disciples allowed the "truth" of their eyes, the "truth" of the situation, and the "truth" of other commentators to override the truth of Christ. Then, as Jesus walked with them along the road to Emmaus, he explained the Scriptures to them and they finally understood.

When seeking truth, do you use your physical senses or your spiritual senses? We need to ask God to open our spiritual eyes, especially when the day of evil comes, so that we can see it clearly and respond to it well.

For we live by faith, not by sight. (2 Cor. 5:7).

What reality will you act on? The devil has a long history of stopping the movement of God's people by getting us to believe a bad report, like the Israelites outside of Canaan. This is something we must always be on our guard against.

An important factor of understanding the truth of God in any situation is to understand our identity in Christ. What happened to me was not because God did not love me. It did not happen because God did not notice what was going on. It was not because God abandoned me. The only way I could be open to seek God's truth in the situation was that I knew he did love me, no matter what the circumstances seemed to be. It was important for me to continually speak out the truth found in Scripture over myself and my life. Again, I want to share a number of Scriptures here to solidify the reality of your relationship with God in your mind.

I am loved by God—I am his child.

Yet to all who did receive him, to those who believed in his name, he gave the right to become children of God. (John 1:12)

For those who are led by the Spirit of God are the children of God. The Spirit you received does not make you slaves, so that you live in fear again; rather, the Spirit you received brought about your adoption to sonship. And by him we cry, "Abba, Father." The Spirit himself testifies with our spirit that we are God's children. (Rom. 8:14–16)

So in Christ Jesus you are all children of God through faith, for all of you who were baptized into Christ have clothed yourselves with Christ. There is neither Jew nor Gentile, neither slave nor free, nor is there male and female, for you are all one in Christ Jesus. If you belong to Christ, then you are Abraham's seed, and heirs according to the promise. (Gal. 3:26–29)

Praise be to the God and Father of our Lord Jesus Christ, who has blessed us in the heavenly realms with every spiritual blessing in Christ. For he chose us in him before the creation of the world to be holy and blameless in his sight. In love he predestined us for adoption to sonship through Jesus Christ, in accordance with his pleasure and will—to the praise of his glorious grace, which he has freely given us in the One he loves. In him we have redemption through his blood, the forgiveness of sins, in accordance with the riches of God's grace that he lavished on us. With all wisdom and understanding. (Eph. 1:3–8)

Nothing can separate me from his love.

I am convinced that neither death nor life, neither angels nor demons, neither the present nor the future, nor any powers, neither height nor depth, nor anything else in all creation, will be able to separate us from the love of God that is in Christ Jesus our Lord. (Rom. 8:38–39)

Jesus is my friend.

"I no longer call you servants, because a servant does not know his master's business. Instead, I have called you friends, for everything that I learned from my Father I have made known to you."
(John 15:15)

God is a good Father.

"Which of you, if his son asks for bread, will give him a stone? Or if he asks for a fish, will give him a snake? If you, then, though you are evil, know how to give good gifts to your children, how much more will your Father in heaven give good gifts to those who ask him!"
(Matt. 7:9–11)

I am accepted by God.

Therefore, since we have been justified through faith, we have peace with God through our Lord Jesus Christ, through whom we have gained access by faith into this grace in which we now stand. And we boast in the hope of the glory of God. (Rom. 5:1–2)

Therefore, there is now no condemnation for those who are in Christ Jesus, because through Christ Jesus the law of the Spirit who gives life has set you free from the law of sin and death. (Rom. 8:1–2)

For he has rescued us from the dominion of darkness and brought us into the kingdom of the Son he loves, in whom we have redemption, the forgiveness of sins. (Col. 1:13–14)

God hears me when I call out to him.

Therefore, since we have a great high priest who has ascended into heaven, Jesus the Son of God, let us hold firmly to the faith we profess. For we do not have a high priest who is unable to empathize with our weaknesses, but we have one who has been tempted in every way, just as we are—yet he did not sin. Let us then approach God's throne of grace with confidence, so that we may receive mercy and find grace to help us in our time of need. (Heb. 4:14–16)

God protects me.

And we know that in all things God works for the good of those who love him, who have been called according to his purpose. (Rom. 8:28)

In him and through faith in him we may approach God with freedom and confidence. (Eph. 3:12)

In all my prayers for all of you, I always pray with joy because of your partnership in the gospel from the first day until now, being confident of this, that he who began a good work in you will carry it on to completion until the day of Christ Jesus. (Phil. 1:4–6)

We know that anyone born of God does not continue to sin; the One who was born of God keeps them safe, and the evil one cannot harm them. (1 John 5:18)

As an heir of heaven, I have authority over the enemy.

The Spirit himself testifies with our spirit that we are God's children. Now if we are children, then we are heirs, heirs of God and co-heirs with Christ, if indeed we share in his sufferings in order that we may also share in his glory. (Rom. 8:16–17)

But because of his great love for us, God, who is rich in mercy, made us alive with Christ even when we were dead in transgressions— it is by grace you have been saved. And God raised us up with Christ and seated us with him in the heavenly realms in Christ Jesus, in order that in the coming ages he might show the incomparable riches of his grace, expressed in his kindness to us in Christ Jesus. (Eph. 2:4–7)

This is the identity to which the enemy wants to blind us. When you read through these Scriptures, the enemy will try to blind you to their truth in your life. You will think of reasons why they are not true for you. This is a spiritual battle, one Paul prayed against.

I pray that the eyes of your heart may be enlightened in order that you may know the hope to which he has called you, the riches of his glorious inheritance in his holy people, and his incomparably great power for us who believe. That power is the same as the mighty strength he exerted when he raised Christ from the dead and seated him at his right hand in the heavenly realms, far above all rule and authority, power and dominion, and every name that is invoked, not only in the present age but also in the one to come. (Eph. 1:18–21)

Paul felt the need to pray for the churches that they would be able to understand the greatness of their place in Christ as sons and daughters of God with full acceptance and a full inheritance, which includes power and authority to have dominion over the enemy in their lives. If your identity in Christ is something you do not feel or accept easily, then read this passage over and over and allow Paul's prayer for the churches to soak into your spirit as a prayer over you.

Eyes to Overcome

The bottom line here is that if you know who you are in Christ, if you know that God loves you, and if you know that God is on your side, then the enemy cannot plant lies in your mind to blame God for your situation and trick you into turning your back on God—the one who loves you and is there to help you.

As I have already stated, if the enemy cannot get you to turn your bitterness toward God, then he will try to focus it on people. But if you choose to walk in forgiveness, then this trick will not work either, and you will focus your anger and blame where it belongs, on the enemy. Then you will stand against him, and you will be able to walk toward freedom.

It was not the fact that my family survived an attack that brought God victory. In fact, that brought him pain. It was what we allowed the Potter to do with the broken pieces that has brought him glory many times over. How you choose to respond to the trial you are facing determines what God can make out of you!

Let me say that again: How you choose to respond to the trial you are facing determines what God can make out of you!

The day of evil can be described as any attack of the enemy that knocks you off course from what God intended for your life and your destiny. But when our eyes are fixed on God and we walk in his truth, no circumstance can destroy us.

Life was not always full of grapes and fine wine for the servants of God in the Bible. David spent fifteen years dwelling in caves and sneaking around behind rocks. He lost everything, and eventually even his own mighty men turned against him at his lowest point. But then he won the entire kingdom. Paul says he experienced times of great abundance and times of great need. But when his eyes were fixed on heaven, he was victorious. Although God does not call us to a life of ease, he does promise victory when we do things his way!

When we look at life one-dimensionally, it is easy to focus on the here and now and how miserable we are because of what so-and-so did. But when we learn to look past this physical dimension, we begin to live life upside down as we view our world through spiritual eyes. Then we begin to see the promises of God at work in our lives, and the hope that is in us becomes a fragrance that enhances our life, permeating each and every life encounter.

There are times in our lives when we become the targets of a full-fledged attack from the enemy. Remember, his aim is total spiritual destruction. He would rather destroy your heart and your spirit and render you useless in the kingdom of God than take your life. What could bring more pain to the heart of the Father than to see his child suffer? The enemy knows that if he can bring enough pain into your life to keep you from ever turning your heart back to God or just leave you bitter enough to spread the venom for him, then he has just increased the size of his army. Whether you know it consciously or not, you will have become a double agent, working for the very enemy who seeks to destroy you!

God created us with the ability to choose. I tell my kids all the time, "How you choose to see this situation will determine the victory you will have." If you do not like the feeling of being sad and upset, then change the story you are telling yourself. This is not about denying the truth. It's about *aligning* with the truth.

I have one child who tends to get hurt feelings by what kids on the playground say to him. Their comments can render him completely useless and diminish him to tears in a moment. This is because God has given him a tender heart. The enemy knows this and uses it to hurl darts at him.

When he shares these struggles with me, I simply ask him, "Is that the truth?" When he shakes his head no, I ask him, "Then why do you let them bother you? If it is not true, then forget about it." We talk about what the truth is. For instance, he is a great athlete and the top of his class. The truth sets him free from the hurtful things that were said over him. We release the opposite of those lies into the spirit realm when we agree on the truth, and this affects his perspective in the natural and ultimately gives him victory.

Our perspective is everything when the day of evil comes: our perspective of ourselves, our perspective of God, our perspective of the situation, our perspective of the future. When tragedy strikes, it affects you deeply spiritually, emotionally, and physically. The only way to walk in freedom is to seek God's perspective. Right perspective will bring truth. Truth will bring hope. And hope will see you through to victory.

Several years ago, I had the opportunity to travel internationally with my parents as they ministered to refugees from the civil war in Serbia. The group with which we worked provided ministry to refugees on both sides of the war. It broke my heart to hear the people on both sides tell similar heartbreaking stories. They were all victims of the same horrific events.

The women told stories of being held captive in rape camps for years at a time. These camps were full of women who were captured after their sons and their husbands were murdered in front of them. Their young daughters were held in these camps with them and continually used for the pleasure of the soldiers. They were held in dungeons and cages and exposed to every type of disease and sickness you can imagine, and they also had to endure seeing their daughters destroyed in front of them.

I can imagine no greater loss or place of hopelessness than these ladies experienced, with their families dead and their homes and lives destroyed. The babies they conceived while incarcerated in these camps were taken from them or killed. When they were finally released, they were rejected by what family they had left because they had been so defiled by enemy soldiers. I have heard other stories of girls, as young as five years old, in other countries being sold by their families for twenty-five dollars as sex slaves.

These horrific existences and terrible tragedies are far beyond what most of us can imagine. But what stood out to me most was that when ministering to these beautiful refugee women, I saw in their eyes a hunger for vengeance and justice. The power that motivated them was hate and revenge. That was stage two of the enemy's plan to destroy them. Trying to help, I shared with them my testimony of forgiveness and prayed that God would use it to shine a ray of hope into the darkness in which they were still held captive.

I could have asked God, "These women have been through so much more than I have; what do I have to say to them? What I went through is nothing compared to them." Instead, I chose to say, "Father, be glorified in my testimony and bring hope to all those who hear. Inspire greatness in these women and release the healing power of forgiveness over their lives."

This is what I shared with the women in Serbia:

> When I was very young, it was hard for me to understand what I was feeling and how to remove the pain from the inside. But I always had the love and support of my family around me. When I was afraid, angry, and did not know what to do, all I needed was to know that they loved me and were always there. They did not always have answers, but they had plenty of love and encouragement. The most important lesson I learned was about forgiveness. For so long I hated our attackers. I wanted to keep hating and get my revenge for what they did to me and my family. The more I would hate, the worse I felt. I would continue to see the images in my head of what they did to us, again and again.
>
> My family encouraged me to forgive, because as long as I hated, those men had power to keep hurting me in my thoughts. They said if I would forgive, that would cut the ties to them and begin to move me away from the constant pain and put me on the path to healing. I really didn't want to do that, because I felt like if I forgave it would be like saying that what they did was okay. It was not okay, it was wrong, and I would be lying to myself if I tried to say it was not.
>
> What I learned was that my forgiveness did not release them from their responsibility or make the trauma

less severe. It only released me from the cycle of constant mental torture. When the pain came, I began to forgive. And each time the feelings would return, I would forgive again until the pain was gone.

My healing began slowly and some days was extremely painful. Then one day I woke up, and the sun was shining in my heart. That's when I found the courage to begin to conquer this mountain in front of me. I had hope again that one day my pain would be gone and I would see joy and happiness.

With the mountaintop as my goal, when those hard days came, I would refuse to give up and to remain in the valley of pain. I wanted to stand on the mountaintop. Today I stand before you on the top of my mountain, and all I see is the beautiful sunrise and the joy that fills my heart.

After the service was over, the women lined up to hug and kiss me. They said, "We will never remember your English name, but we have decided to call you Hope! You have given us hope for our daughters!" I was completely amazed by their tears and sorrow over what I had endured in my dark night. I had no idea my testimony would impact them so deeply, but I praised God for the power of the seed he planted in them that day for forgiveness.

Choosing Peace

"Peace I leave with you; my peace I give you. I do not give to you as the world gives. Do not let your hearts be troubled and do not be afraid." (John 14:27)

Peace is a gift. It is a gift that Jesus left for his church when he finished his earthly ministry. Too many people strain to find their own peace in life amid difficult circumstances. The problem is that there is no peace to be found within our own carnal nature. The peace we seek is something Christ provides for us. To walk in peace, we must seek to receive it from him—which means that our eyes need to be on him and not on ourselves.

This is a choice on our part. From our own basic instincts, we generally focus on ourselves, our feelings, and our problems. Finding peace when it does not come naturally requires a conscious choice. Even more, there are three choices we need to make in succession.

1. We Need to Invite Peace

Although the peace of God is a gift, it does not just fall on us. First, we must invite this peace from God. This is an active seeking, not a passive waiting.

Finally, all of you, be like-minded, be sympathetic, love one another, be compassionate and humble. Do not repay evil with evil or insult with insult. On the contrary, repay evil with blessing, because to this you were called so that you may inherit a blessing. For

"Whoever would love life and see good days must keep their tongue from evil and their lips from deceitful speech. They must turn from evil and do good; they must seek peace and pursue it. For the eyes of the Lord are on the righteous and his ears are attentive to their prayer, but the face of the Lord is against those who do evil." (1 Pet. 3:8–12)

This Scripture passage tells us a few things. It tells us that the eyes of the Lord are on the righteous (those who are in right relationship with God) and that he listens attentively to their requests. One of these requests is to seek peace and pursue it. Jesus says he is leaving us his peace, but we also must pursue it. We do this through prayer, through thanksgiving, and through focusing on God and his goodness above and in spite of our situation.

Do not be anxious about anything, but in everything, by prayer and petition, with thanksgiving, present your requests to God. And the peace of God, which transcends all understanding, will guard your hearts and your minds in Christ Jesus. Finally, brothers, whatever is true, whatever is noble, whatever is right, whatever is pure, whatever is lovely, whatever is admirable—if anything is excellent or praiseworthy—think about such things. (Phil. 4:6–8)

Our natural instinct is to cry out to God for peace and for answers, and then to praise him and thank him when he provides this. However, it is the prayer, praise, and thanksgiving that create the platform for God to show up! We are told that God inhabits the praises of his people (Ps. 22:3). In order to invite the presence of God, which brings peace, we must decide to praise and thank him for his goodness. As we proclaim this, the blocks of the enemy fail and we are able to feel the presence of God that we know has been there all along.

We know God is always with us and will never leave us or forsake us (Deut. 31:6). The problem is that we let the worries of the world and the lies of the enemy cloud our reason and block our ability to feel God's presence and peace. Since we rely so much on feelings, we allow our actions to follow and we act contrary to the ways of the kingdom. So, our task is to ignore our feelings and our temptation to think God is not with us and to proclaim what the word says is true: God is good, he cares for us and loves us, and he is present in our situations. As we proclaim the truth, the truth will set us free. As we resist the lies of the enemy, he must flee (James 4:7).

This is what it means to invite the peace of God. It is to invite the tangible presence of God into our situation. It is not just a simple prayer for Jesus to "come," but a contending invitation in a posture of surrender.

> You will keep in perfect peace those whose minds are steadfast, because they trust in you. (Isa. 26:3)

Will you invite the peace of God into your life?

2. We Need to Accept Peace

Second, when the peace of Christ comes, we need to accept it. This may seem basic and silly. After all, why wouldn't we accept peace if it comes? But to accept the peace of God does not mean to just enjoy some good feelings. The peace of Christ is not just a feeling; it is also instructive. It is a peace requires our active response.

> Let the peace of Christ rule in your hearts, since as members of one body you were called to peace. And be thankful. (Col. 3:15)

To let the peace of Christ rule in our hearts is to let the ways of Christ, the leading of his Spirit, and obedience to his word rule in our hearts. Letting the peace of Christ rule means to let Christ rule in your life without argument, without doubt, and without rebellion. The peace of Christ comes from the decision to trust his ways in our lives.

The peace of Christ will invade and affect our lives only to the degree that we allow it to be instructive and to rule us. Many lose the peace of God because they want to remain in control of their own lives, and they make decisions that run contrary to the way of peace through self-ish, greedy, or vengeful decisions. While we may think these decisions will bring us the peace of perceived justice, they actually bring spiritual darkness. To accept the peace of God also means to accept the Holy Spirit's leading into forgiveness, reconciliation, grace, and mercy.

Peace will be cultivated in our hearts as we focus on and cultivate a deeper relationship with the Spirit of peace within us. He talks to us daily; we just have to slow down and be quiet long enough for him to guide us and bring his peace. We must guard our thoughts against whatever may block his peace from coming to us.

> We demolish arguments and every pretension that sets itself up against the knowledge of God and we take captive every thought to make it obedient to Christ. (2 Cor. 10:5)

> A gentle answer turns away wrath, but a harsh word stirs up anger. (Prov. 15:1)

Will you invite and accept his peace?

3. We Need to Release Peace

Third, we need to release peace into our situation. Again, peace in the kingdom is not just a feeling; it is a way of life. Peace is not passive but active. It is not just something we receive, but something we walk in and spread.

Peace in the kingdom is proactive; it is an offensive weapon to be used. When Jesus was in the boat with the disciples on the Sea of Galilee and the storm came upon them, the disciples saw only the natural situation around them and they became afraid.

> That day when evening came, [Jesus] said to his disciples, "Let us go over to the other side." Leaving the crowd behind, they took him

along, just as he was in the boat. There were also other boats with him. A furious squall came up, and the waves broke over the boat, so that it was nearly swamped. Jesus was in the stern, sleeping on a cushion. The disciples woke him and sad to him, "Teacher, don't you care if we drown?" He got up, rebuked the wind and said to the waves, "Quiet! Be still!" Then the wind died down and it was completely calm. (Mark 4:35–39)

Most versions translate what Jesus said as, "Peace! Be still!" Jesus released the peace within him against the situation and prevailed. The peace within him through the Holy Spirit was stronger than the chaos and fear of the storm around him. And as he released his peace against the storm, the storm gave way.

In this situation, there were twelve scared believers and one man of peace. Today, it is no different. In the church there are many Christians facing difficult situations. For most of them, their first response is to be fearful. When bad things happen in their lives they worry, fume, stress, become angry, hurt, or defensive. They worry all night, complicating their emotional, physical, and spiritual life. They never really walk in peace.

Then there are those men and women of peace. Life comes at them the same as it comes at others around them, yet they are not shaken. They put their trust in God, they release peace into the situation, and they leave their problems with God and get a good night's rest. They then wake refreshed and clear minded to hear and heed the voice and direction of the Spirit. In time, their peace wins out over the situation.

Which one will you be? The peace of God is not stirred by difficult situations. Peace has the power to overcome the world around you. But here is a great key for those who can grasp it:

For peace to work like this in your life, you must go beyond you having peace and allow peace to have you instead.

Beyond our own lives, we are expected to bring peace to the world around us. When Jesus sent out his disciples, he commanded them to extend their peace.

"Go! I am sending you out like lambs among wolves. Do not take a purse or bag or sandals; and do not greet anyone on the road. When you enter a house, first say, 'Peace to this house.' If someone who promotes peace is there, your peace will rest on them; if not, it will return to you." (Luke 10:3–6)

"Whatever town or village you enter, search for some worthy person there and stay at their house until you leave. As you enter the home, give it your greeting. If the home is deserving, let your peace rest on it; if it is not, let your peace return to you." (Matt. 10:11–13)

As with everything in the kingdom of God, we are expected to be conduits, not containers. We grow in the things of God as we release them. Likewise, our peace grows as we release it verbally, relationally, emotionally, and spiritually.

Another point we need to discuss before moving on is that peace and joy are not the same thing. Paul talks about peace and contentment as something that must be learned and something that can be present despite the situation:

I know what it is to be in need, and I know what it is to have plenty. I have learned the secret of being content in any and every situation, whether well fed or hungry, whether living in plenty or in want. (Phil. 4:12)

When the peace of God comes into your situation, it does not necessarily mean that your situation will change right away. Your perspective on the situation will change, however, and you will not be anxious or troubled; instead, you will be able to think clearly and focus on God rather than on your fear. Through prayer, this ability to think clearly and focus on God will often open up responses and solutions you would not have been able to see otherwise, responses and solutions that could very well bring about change in your situation.

Although peace and joy do not always come together, peace will often pave the way for joy to be released. King David knew the peace of God. Whether times were good or bad, David sought the Lord and chose to walk in his peace. As a result, he saw the Lord turn his trials into joy many times.

> You turned my wailing into dancing; you removed my sackcloth and clothed me with joy, that my heart may sing to you and not be silent. Lord my God, I will give you praise forever. (Ps. 30:11–12)

This verse is exactly how I feel. I have felt the wailing, and now I live to dance before the Lord! I have felt spiritually clothed in sackcloth, worthless; but now I live a life clothed with joy. For me, learning to walk in peace means more than just denying my fear. I can deny fear and still be numb. Walking in peace not only denies fear, it restores abundant life. Peace is the inner calm; joy is the outward expression. But joy must be released! In the next chapter, I will talk about how we allow joy to be released in our lives.

Walking in Joy

You may have heard that joy is one of the "fruits" of the Spirit. But what is fruit? It is, of course, the natural product of a tree. An apple tree will naturally produce apples. An orange tree will naturally produce oranges. In the same way, a life yielded to the Spirit and led by the Spirit, as depicted in Romans 8, will naturally produce the fruit of the Spirit.

Too many people attempt to produce the fruits of the Spirit in their own strength. They assess what fruit they are short in, and they apply self-help practices, mental exercises, and personal disciplines to achieve a "breakthrough," but they do so in their own strength. These are all fine practices and tactics, but they must be done in conjunction with seeking a relationship with the Spirit. To do these things in our own strength will bring only frustration (see Paul in Romans 7!).

But when the same things are attempted under the guidance and empowerment of the Holy Spirit through daily prayer and active relationship, they bring forth good fruit naturally (see Paul in Romans 8). Spiritual fruits are not something you can produce. It is the Holy Spirit who produces fruit. This is good news for us! At the same time, it is important to know that you can quench the Holy Spirit and prevent spiritual fruit from ever manifesting in your life as a Christian.

As we follow the Spirit and as fruit develops, we must be open to the continual pruning of the Spirit as well. We need the Holy Spirit to prune away whatever it is that hinders the growth of our fruit and then empower us to make the choices that move us closer to the lifestyle of Christ.

All of this is the point Jesus was making in John 15 as he talked about the vine and the branches. The only way for a branch to be fruitful is to remain in the vine and to be in active contact with the vine. There must be life flowing from the vine into the branch in order for the branch to produce fruit.

The way we remain in the vine is through obedience. As Jesus leads us through his Holy Spirit, we have the choice to obey or not. John 15 tells us that if we continue to obey the commands of Christ, then we will remain in him and in his love. This does not mean he will not love us otherwise; but it does mean that we will not experience the benefit of that love, which leads to fruit. Romans 8:1–17 tells us that if we are led by the Spirit, then we will not fall into the temptations from our sinful nature but will experience the life of the Spirit. After Jesus explained these things in John 15, he told us that this is the path to walking in the fullness of joy:

> "I have told you this so that my joy may be in you and that your joy may be complete." (John 15:11)

Any Christian discussion on joy must address the difference between happiness and joy. For most of the world, the two are synonymous. But for the Christian, there is a stark difference. Happiness is conditioned out of the situation; joy is conditioned out of the heart.

Happiness comes from the world around us, and happiness is often dependent on what is "happening" to us. If people treat us well, if things are going well in our lives, then we are happy. If our circumstances are not favorable, however, then we are unhappy.

Joy comes directly from the Holy Spirit. Joy is a profound, compelling quality of life that transcends the events and disasters that may attack God's people. Joy is a divine dimension of living that is not shackled by circumstances.

In Acts 16, Paul and Silas freed a slave girl from demonic oppression. As a result, her ability to tell fortunes for her owners went away. The slave girl's owners were so angry they had Paul and Silas arrested, stripped, beaten, thrown in jail, and chained to the wall. Yet there in the inner cell of this prison, they began to pray and sing out hymns to God. Pretty soon, the entire prison was shaken, the doors flew open, and everyone's chains fell off. The presence of God fell upon that place. Physical salvation came to Paul and Silas, and spiritual salvation came to the jailer and his household. Peace in their spirits led to joy in the situation.

Look at what they did here. Paul and Silas had learned the secret of being content in all situations. Therefore, they experienced the fruit of the joy of the Spirit in their hearts despite their dire situation. Because of this inner reality, they chose to look past their situation and invite the peace of God by praising him and singing to him despite their natural feelings. This created the spiritual foundation for the tangible presence of God to break through the enemy's lines and shake up their situation. The change in their situation brought glory to God and led to the physical happiness of all involved.

So, what made them sing? Joy. Paul and Silas may not have been happy to be in prison, but they were able to pray and sing. The word used for prayer here is not a prayer of supplication. Paul and Silas were not praying, "Please get us out of this mess!" The word used here is for a prayer of praise or worship. They were not crying for help; they were commenting on how good God is. This was to be a lifestyle for Paul:

> Therefore, since we have been justified through faith, we have peace with God through our Lord Jesus Christ, through whom we have gained access by faith into this grace in which we now stand. And we boast in the hope of the glory of God. Not only so, but we also glory in our sufferings, because we know that suffering produces perseverance; perseverance, character; and character, hope. And hope does not put us to shame, because God's love has been poured out into our hearts through the Holy Spirit, who he has given to us. (Rom. 5:1–5)

Why would Paul rejoice in suffering and perseverance? Because Paul was a warrior and warriors understand that there is honor and joy in the elite corps. Have you ever watched a documentary on an Army Ranger school or a Navy Seal school? It is quite difficult. There is much suffering and perseverance, yet there is still a fire in the hearts and eyes of those involved and a joy in the process of becoming part of an elite fighting team.

Paul had a clear spiritual perspective. He understood that there is great reward in heaven when we endure here on earth.

"Blessed are you when people insult you, persecute you and falsely say all kinds of evil against you because of me. Rejoice and be glad, because great is your reward in heaven, for in the same way they persecuted the prophets who were before you." (Matt. 5:11–12)

Rather, as servants of God we commend ourselves in every way: in great endurance; in troubles, hardships and distresses; in beatings, imprisonments and riots; in hard work, sleepless nights and hunger; in purity, understanding, patience and kindness; in the Holy Spirit and in sincere love; in truthful speech and in the power of God; with weapons of righteousness in the right hand and in the left; through glory and dishonor, bad report and good report; genuine, yet regarded as impostors; known yet regarded as unknown; dying and yet we live on; beaten and yet not killed, sorrowful yet always rejoicing; poor yet making many rich; having nothing and yet possessing everything. (2 Cor. 6:4–10)

This does not sound like a formula for joy, and yet over and over again Paul writes about joy in the strangest circumstances. Why were Paul and Silas able to sing and praise God while they were locked away in prison? They knew they mattered to God. When you get to the place where you can understand that you matter to the Master of the Universe, then you are on your path to joy. In Matthew, Jesus told his followers this:

"Are not two sparrows sold for a penny? Yet not one of them will fall to the ground outside your Father's care. And the very hairs on your head are all numbered. So don't be afraid; you worth more than many sparrows." (Matt.10:29–31)

Paul and Silas knew they mattered to God, and they knew they had angered the owners of the slave girl. But they also knew that pleasing man was not what they were called to do. There is nothing in this world that will steal your joy as quickly as trying to please everyone. You cannot do it. Not even God can please everyone, and he's God! If we try to please everyone, it will destroy us. If pleasing everyone becomes our goal, we will never feel joy. We will constantly live with the fear of failing someone.

In my ministry as a pastor's wife and as a speaker, I do not teach to please people; I teach to please God. I say what I feel God wants me to say, not what I think you want to hear. If I make people happy when I teach, then great. It is not my goal to offend; but if some get offended, I do not let it bother me because I am going to be able to stand before God with a clear conscience.

In life, people constantly evaluate you. Your boss has expectations of you as an employee, children expect certain things of you as a parent, and parents expect things from you as their son or daughter. If you are going to live your life trying to please everyone, then you are destined to live a joyless, self-destructive life.

You need to realize that you are to receive your identity, your rewards, and your joy from God. Paul and Silas knew their imprisonment was just a minor hiccup in their lives. They knew that God was in control and that ultimately he wins. It may have appeared that God had deserted them, but we have already seen that this was not true: they mattered to God. And they knew that no matter what happened, God had a plan. After all, it was Paul who wrote:

And we know that in all things God works for the good of those who love him, who have been called according to his purpose. (Rom. 8:28)

Paul and Silas knew they loved God, and they knew they were called according to his purpose for them. So they were able to be confident that everything was going to work together for their good, even if they did not understand when or how.

I know we go through seasons in life when being joyful is difficult, if not impossible. But I also know that it will pass. Every night has a dawn, every storm has an end, and every mountain has a crest. King David struggled with depression throughout his life (just read the psalms), but he also had a grip on this joy thing. Listen to what he wrote in Psalm 30:5, "Weeping may go on all night, but joy comes with the morning."

If your joy is based on circumstances, then you need to give your life over to the Lord and let him place his joy within you.

The Joy Thief

Our enemy, the devil, knows all about joy and is determined to steal our joy and peace if he can, and he does so slowly. He creeps into our lives with subtle lies and quiet temptations; and in our busy lives, we don't realize this is happening until one day we wake up and realize our joy is gone and we don't know how to get it back.

But the Spirit knows all. If we want to see the fruit of joy ripen in our lives, we need the Holy Spirit to prune away whatever steals our joy and focus us on whatever feeds our joy. However, we must also be able to recognize the attacks of the enemy soon enough to turn to the Spirit for help. In 2 Corinthians 2:11, Paul says that one of the reasons he did not get sidetracked by the enemy was that he was not unaware of the enemy's schemes. The more we know the common schemes of the devil for stealing our joy, the more readily we will be able to combat those schemes with the peace of Christ.

Here are some of the most common joy stealers that can keep our fruit of joy from producing and ripening.

Unmet Expectations

Maybe your life is not going the way you planned. Maybe your expectations for your marriage have not been met. Or maybe your kids are not living like they should.
Perhaps you do not have everything you want, such as a bigger house, a nicer car, or a better job.

> I know what it is to be in need, and I know what it is to have plenty. I have learned the secret of being content in any and every situation, whether well fed or hungry, whether living in plenty or in want. (Phil. 4:12)

Paul calls contentment a "secret." He also had to "learn" how to live with unsatisfied expectations. Likewise, we must learn to live with plenty or with little. Contentment does not come when we have everything we want, but when we are satisfied with everything we have.

Do you have unsatisfied expectations that have led to a spirit of discontentment in your life? If so, you need to determine to do whatever it takes to learn the secret of wanting everything you have and not necessarily having everything you want. When you do this, you will begin to experience joy in even the small things of life. Confess your discontent to the Lord right now. There is freedom in this path!

Fear of Losing What You Have (Greed)

Greed (or fear of loss) will cause you to hold on to what you have too tightly. There is no possibility of risk in your life when there is fear of loss. You will not risk anything for God and his kingdom if you are afraid you may lose something precious from your personal kingdom. But risk is where advancement lies. You will hoard things you never use, because you do not want to waste the money to buy them again. You will always worry about whether you could have gotten a better deal, rather than enjoy the fact that you just blessed someone else. Your possessions will rule you and steel your joy.

Unresolved Conflict

When we hold on to offenses in our lives, we cannot have joy. Offenses feed bitterness in our souls, and bitterness and joy cannot co-exist. Offenses also have a way of occupying most of our free mental and emotional attention. Think about the last major offense you suffered. How often did you replay the offense in your mind? How much of your conversation with others focused on that offense? When our attention is so focused on the wrongdoing of others in our lives, we have little attention left for focusing on the Lord.

> Make every effort to live in peace with all men and to be holy; without holiness no one will see the Lord. See to it that no one falls short of the grace of God and that no bitter root grows up to cause trouble and defile many. (Heb. 12:14–15)

Are you involved in some conflict with someone? If so, confess it to God and make plans to meet with that person face-to-face, if possible, so that you can become reconciled and get back on your journey to joy. If reconciliation is not possible, then choose to let go of bitterness anyway: forgive.

Unconfessed Sin

Guilt can kill your joy faster than anything I know. Anytime we have sin in our lives, the enemy assaults us with condemnation and guilt. This blocks the joy of God from working in our lives. When we follow the conviction of the Holy Spirit and confess our sins, turning back to God's path, we are forgiven and his joy and blessings can be experienced in our lives.

Blessed is the one whose transgressions are forgiven, whose sins are covered. Blessed is the one whose sin the Lord does not count against them and in whose spirit is no deceit. When I kept silent, my bones wasted away through my groaning all day long.

> For day and night your hand was heavy on me; my strength was sapped as in the heat of summer. Then I acknowledged my sin to you and did not cover up my iniquity. I said, "I will confess my transgressions to the Lord"— and you forgave the guilt of my sin." (Ps. 32:1–5)

When we confess our sins and do our best to walk in obedience, we are restored into right relationship with God, or what the Bible calls righteousness. Righteousness is not some position of super-spirituality that only a few ultra-godly people can attain. Righteousness is right-ness. It is doing your best to live right before God. When we live our lives this way, the devil has no sin to hold over us and convict us of. Therefore, we are free in spirit to experience God's joy and his peace in our lives.

> Rejoice in the Lord and be glad, you righteous; sing, all you who are upright in heart! (Ps. 32:11)

David was one of the people in the Old Testament known for his joy in the Lord. This was one of his major strengths. Yet even David was not able to experience that joy until he confessed his sins.

> Cleanse me with hyssop, and I will be clean; wash me, and I will be whiter than snow. Let me hear joy and gladness; let the bones you have crushed rejoice. (Ps. 51:7–8)

Is the weight of the Lord heavy on you because you are not answering the Holy Spirit's conviction in your life? Confess your sins, repent, and you will be forgiven, and you too will once again feel the fruit of joy in your life.

As a result of discontentment, conflict, and open sin, David had flattened out spiritually. His joy was a long-lost memory until he acknowledged his wrongdoing and repented. This enabled him to come before God, asking, "Restore to me the joy of your salvation" (Ps. 51:12). Likewise, when we confess our sin and allow the Lord to cleanse us, our joy can also be restored.

Joy Builders

Not only must we avoid and overcome joy stealers, we must actively concentrate on engaging joy builders. Here are some examples.

Realize That God Rejoices Over You

We can be helped greatly in our journey toward joy if we learn to see the Almighty not as a taskmaster, but as the God of the universe with joy in his heart.

> The Lord your God is with you, the Mighty Warrior who saves. He will take great delight in you, in his love he will no longer rebuke you, but will rejoice over you with singing. (Zeph. 3:17)

> But be glad and rejoice forever in what I will create, for I will create Jerusalem to be a delight and its people a joy. I will rejoice over Jerusalem and take delight in my people; the sound of weeping and of crying will be heard in it no more. (Isa. 65:18–19)

If we have little or no joy in our lives, it could very well be because we do not know God well enough. Joy is one of his character qualities! When we recognize God as joyful, we will be even more drawn to him and we will feel the presence of his joy.

God is not a distant judge waiting for us to mess up so he can unleash his fury. He has created us to be his delight. He finds great joy in you! He rejoices over you in happy song.

As we view God this way, we will discover that he takes great pleasure in us.

"The joy of the Lord is your strength" (Neh. 8:10).

Stay Connected to the Body
The first joy builder is vertical and has to do with how we view God and how he views us. Connection to God is paramount! But our relationship with other believers is also important for our joy. God created us to live in community and to share his love and joy with one another.

> Convinced of this, I know that I will remain, and I will continue with all of you for your progress and joy in the faith, so that through my being with you again your boasting in Christ Jesus will overflow on account of me. (Phil. 1:25–26)

As I connect with you and you connect with me, our joy grows, resulting in greater connection with God. Joy is contagious and is something we can share back and forth. We need each other. If we are not attending church on a regular basis, or if we attend church but don't interact with others, then we rob ourselves of joy.

When we live in loving relationships with our brothers and sisters in Christ, we then experience more joy ourselves and we can help others experience our joy.

The best way I know for this to happen is for everyone to be involved in small-group relationships. As we gather with other believers for accountability, growth, prayer, and study, God will use each of us to raise the joy around us.

Give Your Worries to God
One of the hallmarks of Christian joy is that it can be experienced in the midst of intense sorrow and loss. Often we define happiness as the absence of something undesirable, such as pain, suffering, or disappointment. But Christian joy is the proper response to the presence

of something desirable: God himself. This was the view of Paul and Silas in jail.

The only way to have an attitude like this is to release our problems to the Lord. Because we know that God is in charge, we can have joy no matter what happens. Even amid trials, troubles, and tribulations in the physical world, in our spirits, we can experience the joy that we have fostered in the Lord.

I have spoken to you with great frankness; I take great pride in you. I am greatly encouraged; in all our troubles my joy knows no bounds. (2 Cor. 7:4)

Consider it pure joy, my brothers and sisters, whenever you face trials of many kinds. (James 1:2)

This takes a conscious decision. We are commanded to work at it. Besides, what is the worst that could happen to us as Christians? We could die and be with the Lord. Not so bad!

Learn to Enjoy Life (Be Present)

Here is a growth challenge: read through the book of Philippians every day for a week. The word *joy* or *rejoice* is used nineteen different times in this short book. As you read it, ask God to ripen the fruit of joy in your life through the Holy Spirit.

For the kingdom of God is not a matter of eating and drinking, but of righteousness, peace, and joy in the Holy Spirit. (Rom. 14:17)

This verse shows a solid progression. Righteousness means rightness. It means being in a right place with God and knowing your place with God. This is a prerequisite for peace. If you don't know who you are or how God feels about you, then you cannot have peace in the relationship. Peace, as I mentioned before, is the foundation of joy. Peace is the inner calm, and joy is the outward expression. The enemy understands this and will try to rob your joy by pulling the rug out from under it. If he can disrupt your righteousness through sin or doubt, he will. We guard against this by remaining in the word, in prayer, and in fellowship with the body. If he cannot disrupt your righteousness, then he will try to disrupt your peace.

The storms of life are distractions brought by the enemy in an attempt to get our focus off of Jesus and onto the world, undermining our peace and robbing us of our joy. Peace is simply the ability to stay focused on Jesus, no matter what is happening around you. It is the ability to still the worries of your mind, to look past them and find God's presence in the moment.

"Be still and know that I am God." (Ps. 46:10)

The Hebrew word for "be still" means "to ease up" or "let go." When you are driving, if you take a corner too fast, you could lose control, you could wreck your car, and you could get injured. As a result, we know that when we approach a sharp corner, we should ease up on the gas to allow for proper control through the corner.

As we approach problems in life, corners we cannot see around, God wants us to ease up ("be still") and make sure we have proper control in the curve ("know that he is God"). In this, his peace guides us through our situation. So many of our problems in life come because of our inability to ease up and trust God.

Continuing in Peace through Presence

All fruitfulness in our lives flows from the place of intimacy with the Lord. The kingdom of darkness is aimed at getting us to focus on something other than God, because our communion with him is the power source of our lives and connects us with the eternal purpose of our life on this planet! When it comes to joy, it is imperative that we live in the peace of the presence of God. Lack of peace will steal our joy.

Is it possible that the enemy knows our job better than we do? He knows that our task, if we are walking in our position of delegated authority, is to destroy his works. The power of the superior kingdom in us will destroy the inferior kingdom of the enemy in our circumstances. But we can only release that kingdom to the degree that our hearts and minds are in agreement with it. We can only be in agreement with it if we are connected to it. So, to keep us disconnected and thus ineffective, our enemy uses lies and fear to make the problems we face appear bigger than the solutions we carry.

Do we believe the Scripture that "all things are possible" or that "if the Lord is on my side who can be against me"? If we truly believe these things, they will be at work in our lives to the point that the devil can no longer convince us that our situation is hopeless or bigger than the reality of God's kingdom.

King David was tested when he entered circumstances that directly contradicted God's word over his life. It was prophesied he would be king, yet he lived for many years as a fugitive. He was brought into the court of the king, only to be driven out and hunted. His job was to ignore the enemy's agenda and develop the strength of character that God desired in him. The strongest test of this is recorded in 1 Samuel 24, when it appeared the God had delivered Saul into David's hands in the cave near En Gedi. All of his men believed this and prodded him to kill Saul. Yet I believe that in his heart, David knew this was not God's will and that the enemy would use this against him, so he spared Saul's life, which was a move of great character in that age.

Joseph discovered this as well. As he came into his destiny, he saw that God's purpose had a momentum and power that outweighed the evil plan of his brothers. He said, "You intended to harm me, but God intended it for good to accomplish what is now being done, the saving of many lives" (Gen. 50:20). Joseph's statement here does not deny the reality that his brothers made choices that affected his life; but instead of focusing on the negativity of his situation, he instead focused on the superior reality of God that their plans could not overcome. In fact, their evil intentions became the very tools that God used to bring Joseph into his promotion and the ultimate fulfillment of God's promise.

In the end, Joseph was called the greatest man in all of Egypt, second only to Pharaoh. Joseph was not defined by his failure as a prideful, boasting brother, or by his fall into a life of slavery through the wickedness of his brothers, or by the false accusation of rape and his life as a convict. In all of these things, Joseph allowed God to lead him. He looked for the good; he honored and praised God and sought joy in his circumstances. He chose to walk in the peace of God and in forgiveness. In each situation, Joseph was defined by his integrity and by his walk with God. And in the end, Joseph was defined by the power of his great God working through him.

It is the oil of God's presence that gives me everything I need, anointing me to fulfill my purpose. But he only gives me the measure of his presence that I am willing to jealously guard. So I have to build my strength of will and character to focus all my energies on carrying his presence and peace with excellence. I cannot afford to have a moment in my life when the circumstances distract me from tending that fire in my heart.

While God does not create the evil situations in our lives, he is not defeated by them either. Evil does not limit his ability to bring about the fulfillment of all that he has purposed to do in us. We see this in the life of King David. We see this in the life of Joseph. We see this in the life of Paul and the apostles. I have seen it in my own life. But God is also not limited by what we have or what we can do. Nobody starts out as a spiritual giant. David started as a shepherd in a field with a staff. He didn't have much with him out in the field. But what he had, he gave to God. In the next chapter, I would like to ask you one question: What's in your hand, and will you let God use it?

What Is in Your Hand?

The point of this book is not to help those who read it overcome their past. That is definitely a part of this book, but it is not the point, the main goal. I have seen many people overcome their past but then do nothing for God afterward. My goal in this book and in sharing my story is to release those who read it into productive ministry. For many, this means first overcoming the traps and snares of the enemy that are holding them back. Second, it means empowering them with the truths and the mind-set to live in freedom and victory. But, third, it means prodding them to get out there and join in the mission of Christ, to bring that same freedom and victory to others (Isa. 61:1; Luke 4:18; John 10:10).

God continues to stir in my heart the concept of "What is in your hand?" We do not necessarily need any special training, ability, background, or circumstances to be used by God. He can use whatever you are already carrying with you to do great things. In that way, God is kind of like the 1980s television character MacGyver.

A great example of this is found in the story of Moses when God asked him to lead the people of Israel out of slavery in Egypt. This meant going toe-to-toe with one of the most powerful leaders of one of the most powerful kingdoms on earth, the Pharaoh of Egypt. To bring the people of Israel out of slavery in Egypt would mean either a physical battle against the Egyptian army (Moses had no army to lead), a power encounter against the great sorcerers and magicians of Egypt (Moses had no training in mystical arts), a clever deception masterfully planned out (Moses did not feel overly cunning), or an artful and convincing debate (Moses did not feel good with words). Moses was given a great task that really needed, by human standards, a great person, well trained and well equipped to carry it out. But God had a different plan.

God appeared to Moses at the burning bush and explained what he wanted Moses to do. Moses' first task, even before approaching Pharaoh, would be to convince the people of Israel to follow him when the time came. Again, his background and training were all wrong. He was not one of them that they should listen to him. He had been raised as an Egyptian, and he was also a known murderer. In addition, he had been AWOL for many years in hiding. There was no reason in the natural reality for Moses to have any confidence that the Israelite leaders would listen to him at all.

Do you ever feel inadequate for a task? Do you ever feel like you do not know the Bible well enough to speak to people about God? What about speaking in front of a group or a whole church? Do the challenges in this book seem too much for you? Do you feel that because of something in your past, you cannot be used by God? That you are broken? That you have too much baggage? That you are unimportant and unworthy? Then great! Welcome to the life of Moses, one of the greatest leaders in the Bible!

So how did God take this broken, embarrassed, guilty, lonely man and make him victorious over everything in his life? Did he give him great gifts? Did he enlighten his mind with great wisdom? No, he simply used the common, everyday things that Moses had with him already.

> Moses questioned God, asking, "What if they do not believe me or listen to me and say, 'The Lord did not appear to you'?" But God did not address any of Moses' concerns. He merely asked, "What is in your hand?" (Exod. 4:2).

In Moses' hand was a simple staff, nothing fancy. Yet at the command of the Lord God, it transformed into a snake when Moses laid it down, and it transformed back into a staff when he took it back up. God was showing Moses that it did not matter to him what little Moses had to offer. Even a simple staff could bring miraculous results, if offered up in faith and obedience to God.

What is in your hand?

What about Jesus' disciples when the crowds that followed them became hungry? Mark and John give the more detailed versions of the story. It was late in the afternoon, and the people were hungry. The disciples encouraged Jesus to send the people away into the towns so they could buy food. But Jesus replied to the disciples, "You give them something to eat." Wow. That is a big task! The crowd was at least five thousand men, plus all the women and children. This was an overwhelming request. The disciples' first reply was much like Moses'. They did not feel ready or equipped for such a task. They said to Jesus, "Even eight month's wages would not be enough for everyone to have a bite." Jesus, however, did not address their concerns. He merely asked them, "What do you have? Go and see."

There was a boy among them who had five small barley loaves and two small fish. It was nothing much considering the crowd. Yet at the command of the Lord, it miraculously multiplied in their baskets and fed everyone there, with twelve baskets full of leftovers. Jesus showed the disciples that it did not matter to him what little the disciples had to offer. Even a few loaves and fish could bring miraculous results, if offered up in faith and obedience to God.

What is in your hand?

One of the most powerful items in the Old Testament was the Ark of the Covenant. Do you remember what the ark contained? It contained the tablets of the law, a jar of manna, and the staff of Aaron that budded. The law represented the living word of God. The manna represented God's provision. The staff represented the power of God.

It is the combination of these same three things in our lives that make us a force with which to be reckoned. When we are in covenant with God, he makes his dwelling place in us. We become the Ark of the Covenant. In the Great Commission, Jesus called his church to go forth into the world, boldly proclaiming his word, lovingly sharing his provision, and faithfully displaying his power to a hurt, lost, and dying world that needed him. It does not matter how little you may think you have to offer. These things dwell inside of you through the Holy Spirit and are ready to manifest themselves through you if you will give them but the slightest chance.

Will you step out in boldness? Will you stop worrying about everything you lack and every way that you fall short? Will you stop letting your past freeze you in the moment? Will you look to see what you do have? What is in your hand?

When I ask you that question, it is with the firm belief that God can win with any hand! The story I shared with you about my family is not something that defines my life. It is a story of how I got through one difficult night and the aftereffects of that night. My testimony is the story of God's glory being revealed in and through my life as a result of my willingness to submit to his love time and again. My testimony is not about a bad night that was the result of a bad decision on the part of other people who were under the influence of the enemy. It is about the love and faithfulness God had for me during that time, the protection he brought me and my family that night, the restoration he brought to us over the years, the love and glory he revealed to me through the process of recovery, and the power he has witnessed in and through me since. I am not defined by an attack of the enemy. I am defined by the grace, love, and power of my God.

Your testimony is not about the worst thing that ever happened to you, unless you allow that thing to define you. If you allow God into that part of your life story and give him control of everything related to it (your perceptions, bitterness, sorrow, anger, resentment), then he will refine you into pure gold and your life into one of victory. It is your choice. Your life can be a tragedy or a testimony.

I believe testimonies are important. They are the power we have over areas of darkness in our lives. When I share the goodness of God in my life, it releases the truth of God's deep love for his children. And when that truth is released, it becomes the power to create the next miracle. The Holy Spirit uses our testimonies to build faith and hope in others who still walk that road, and it releases love into their hearts through revealed truth.

What is your story? Is it a story of good news and hope? Or is it a tale of tragedy and sorrow? Do most of your words bring fear of the enemy by extolling his victories in your life? Or do most of your words bring glory to God for his work in your life?

The Scriptures tell us that out of the heart, the mouth speaks. If the words we speak to ourselves or others do not bring the power and glory of God into our situation, then this is a sign that we are allowing ourselves to remain fixated in our hearts on the wrong thoughts. If we want to see the enemy continue to control us through fear and doubt, then all we have to do is keep thinking about the bad side of life. But if we want God's love and presence, peace and joy, and victory to fill our lives, then we need to change the meditations of our hearts. We need to focus on Jesus and his love, goodness, joy, and peace.

> May these words of my mouth, and this meditation of my heart, be pleasing in your sight, Lord, my Rock and my Redeemer. (Ps. 19:14)

Focusing on Jesus is the first step to becoming a weapon of mass destruction against the enemy! Fix your eyes on Jesus, the author and finisher of your faith, and take every thought captive to the obedience of Christ.

> We demolish arguments and every pretension that sets itself up against the knowledge of God, and we take captive every thought to make it obedient to Christ. (2 Cor. 10:5)

Now you have the foundation to put yourself in a position to begin to use everything in your life to your advantage.

God has gifted each and every one of us with unique and specific weapons to fire into the enemy camp. Love is the strongest of all of them. I heard a story recently about a lady who made cupcakes every week. Every Friday for a year, she took these cupcakes to a local brothel.

She did not go in preaching or condemning, just carrying cupcakes. After a year, the first girl gave her heart to the Lord. When she was asked why, she said it was all because of the cupcakes! She felt loved by the cupcake lady in a way no one had ever loved her before. She knew that the love had to come from somewhere, and she wanted to know why the cupcake lady had so much love!

You might say, "I don't have a testimony like she does." Or "I'm not musically gifted." Or "I can't write a book." The list can go on and on. But can you make cupcakes? As long as we focus on what we do not have or cannot do, we cannot reach our full potential and destiny. We can only go on living a mediocre life, talking about the great things others have been gifted to do.

The things in your life that hold you back and that you regret are the very things that, when submitted to God, can bring him glory and you honor. What is the difference between a common grain of sand and a valuable pearl? Or between a lump of coal and a diamond? It is the environment to which they are subjected. If we take the common lumps of coal in our lives and submit them to the environment of the Holy Spirit, he will produce something of great value. There may be some pressure involved, but it is for a greater purpose.

I want to challenge you to seek whatever God has designed you for that is so much bigger than you, the thing you feel unworthy and completely unqualified to do. For me it was writing a book. I would say to you that if you can accomplish the dream you have on your own, then it may be too small. There is nothing supernatural about it. But if the dream you have is equivalent to feeding five thousand people with five loaves and two fish, then you are on the right track.

Maybe you have buried the dream because you tried and it failed. It may be time to try again. But what if you fail again? Then try again after that. Edison failed over two thousand times in his attempt to invent the lightbulb. When questioned about it later, he said that he did not fail two thousand times at making the lightbulb. He successfully determined one thousand, nine hundred and ninety-nine ways not to make a lightbulb! That attitude is what led him to keep trying, eventually bringing him to the one try that worked and brought light to the whole world.

What is in your hand? It's time to hope again and live this life to the fullest!

The Importance of Worship

"Yet a time is coming and has now come when the true worshipers will worship the Father in the Spirit and in truth, for they are the kind of worshipers the Father seeks. God is spirit, and his worshipers must worship in the Spirit and in truth." (John 4:23–24)

In this book, I have shared a lot of how-to advice from my experience on things such as taking thoughts captive, walking in power and authority, and choosing peace and joy. These are all solid biblical principles that helped move me from victim to victor. As I reflect upon my journey, however, I know that none of these would have gained the fruit in my life that they did without the spirit of worship that surrounded them. Worship is the foundation for victory!

Worship is the essence of a relationship that goes beyond religion. It was my relationship with my God that brought me through my struggles. Mere disciplines of religion would not have worked. It is not my desire to teach you how to worship. That is the job of the Holy Spirit and your church. My desire is to share my testimony of the power and place of worship that propelled my life into abundance and destiny. I will be direct in saying that you cannot get to that place without an understanding of true worship.

The strongholds of the enemy in my life, those places where I was stuck and beaten down, were torn down through worship. It was through worship that I felt the love of the Father. It was this love, experienced in worship, that gave me the courage to overcome the spirit of fear that masqueraded as the man in black. It was worship that focused my mind on the truth and helped me overcome the nightmares and flashbacks that had overwhelmed me. Also, the night that changed everything for me, the night I saw the face of Jesus in a vision, came from a place of worship.

Every chapter of this book has come from a place of worship. Without the foundation of worship, everything written here is just an exercise of the mind and the works of the flesh. Without the empowerment of God through the Holy Spirit in our lives, all of these things will fall flat. This is the focus of Romans 8. Under the leading of the Holy Spirit, we are free to overcome the enemy in our lives.

Worship Is Relationship

Real worship is the difference between religion and relationship. Although religion may make us feel better about ourselves, it brings little real power. A real relationship with God brings the presence of God into our lives, and it is that presence that overcomes the enemy.

Now, anyone can "practice" worship as a form of religion. But just as true, anyone can experience it as true relationship. If worship is viewed only as a few songs that we sing on Sunday morning before the sermon, then it is probably an act of religion. Of course, I understand that everyone must start somewhere. For all of us, worship starts as a discipline in which we must learn and gro. The key here is that we are indeed growing in it. It starts on Sunday morning in the community gathering. But as it grows, and as it changes from religious exercise into relational connection, then it breaks out of the walls of the church and we begin to worship in our car as we drive, worship as we walk or jog through the neighborhood, and worship as part of our quiet times. In time, worship becomes a lifestyle.

When worship becomes a lifestyle and not just a discipline, it produces tremendous fruit in our lives. As we develop a lifestyle of worship, we become aware of God's presence all day, in everything we do. We invite that presence to be a part of us as we go throughout our day. The enemy, the devil and his minions, cannot stand against the presence of God, and the presence of his light around us causes the darkness to flee.

God is always around us, everywhere. But many Christians fail to tap into that presence. Worship is not some mystical ritual of breaking into some higher realm, it is simply the decision to recognize the presence of God and the other realm Jesus called the kingdom of heaven, which is already around us.

Worship begins as a discipline in our lives as a response to the command of Scripture for us to worship the Lord our God; and as we obey this command, our lives are transformed as worship becomes something we cherish.

Worship Is Learned

I mentioned that for most, worship begins on Sunday morning and then breaks out of the walls of the church. This is because although we were created for worship, the enemy has so clouded our minds that worship is not natural for us in the context of this sinful world. As a result, we need to learn how to worship. For most, that learning begins on Sunday mornings. For others, like me, it is learned in the home.

In my life, worship was modeled for me on a daily basis by my parents. It was never just a thing we did on Sunday morning at church. It was something that filled our home to the point that I had no idea it was not normal. My mom sang over our home night and day. I could always find her in our house by following the sound of her praise. She created an atmosphere of peace in our home through her worship.

Often, we would worship as a family. Through my parents' worship I could feel the presence of God in the room, even at a young age. It was a sweet presence of peace and joy and love. It was a presence I wanted more of in my life. In time, I sought and found this presence for myself, but I learned it first through joining in worship with my parents.

This is why it is important to join in corporate worship sessions, even if you do not feel anything at first. Corporate worship, if it is true worship led by worship leaders and not mere song leaders, is designed to invite the presence of God into the corporate body of the church. A good, strong church will be filled with saints of God, elders in the faith who have strong relationships with God. As they worship together, the presence of the Holy Spirit descends upon the place. It does not matter if it is a Catholic Mass or a Pentecostal prayer meeting. True worship is a matter of the heart, not of any particular form. When the Spirit of God falls on a group of worshipers, even those not matured in worship have the benefit of feeling his presence. This opens the door for them to learn deeper personal worship.

When Paul and Silas were in jail and began to worship late into the night, the presence of the Lord fell upon the jail so powerfully that the place shook, chains fell off the prisoners, and all the doors flew open. That is amazing. But even more amazing is that none of the other prisoners left the place. Imagine that. They were locked in a dark, cold dungeon. They were probably malnourished and weary. Some had probably been there a long time. Here was their big chance to escape. Why didn't they run? Because they felt something in their spirits through Paul and Silas's worship that was more important to them than their physical freedom. They felt the presence of God through someone else's worship.

In the same way, anyone who does not know how to worship or invite the presence of God on their own can learn to do so by sitting in the presence of those who do. This is why the choice of church is so important. I highly encourage you to make true worship a main priority for church selection, not just good teaching or kids' programs. And good worship does not just mean energetic songs. There are a lot of worship services that appear lively but have no presence of God within them. Paul refers to this in 2 Timothy 3:5 as having the appearance of godliness but denying its power, and thus having no life within. When you sit in worship, listen with your spirit. Do you feel anything different in this place? Realize that it may take a few times visiting a church to feel the real heart. But my encouragement is to look with your spirit, not just your emotions and your mind.

Aside from the main, Sunday morning worship time, look for smaller group worship nights. It is usually the more mature and more intentional who take the time to come to church on days other than Sunday. These gatherings often—not always, but often—may have a stronger presence of God due to the presence of mature worshipers in a more intimate setting.

In time, as we begin to fully comprehend what true worship is, it becomes for us a lifeline, a direct connection to the very throne room of heaven. It becomes our greatest privilege and gift. It becomes an intimate connection with our loving Father. There is a difference between corporate worship and personal worship, but there is a place for both. Just as married people display their love for each other differently in public than in private, there is a different expression of worship for God in private than in public. I do love the supercharged power that comes from corporate worship and I would never trade that; but when I worship alone, I am completely uninhibited. For me, to really enter a deep place of worship with the Lord, I prefer to be alone.

Worship Is Warfare

There is no greater tool against the enemy than worship! As I mentioned, Mom contended for peace and victory in our home through her worship. I praise God for the lifestyle of worship she modeled for us. She taught me how to sing with my spirit, not just my voice. That lifestyle of worship was demonstrated in both the mountaintops and in the valleys of my life. True worship does not depend on our circumstances, but it has the capacity to transform our circumstances.

Many people worship God only when they feel like it, because of their positive circumstances. But when times get hard, they have a hard time worshiping. Yet the Bible tells us in Philippians 4 that we are to give praise in all things. *All things.* Why? Because if hard times fall on us or if the enemy attacks us, the only thing that can make things better is the presence of God. Worship invites that presence. When even in a bad situation we choose to worship, we invite God's presence, we transform our thinking, and we step into our authority. Then the enemy's power is broken and he flees. It is like calling in the cavalry. So instead of being a response to the situations in our lives, worship is what creates and transforms the situations of our lives.

You may remember earlier when I said that when Mom was rescued from her captors, the men who picked her up reported that she was singing. I know they thought she had lost her mind, but the spiritual reality was that this singing they heard was what kept her sane. She was not merely singing; she was doing warfare in the spirit realm, contending for herself and her family. When her darkest hour fell heavy upon her, deep called out to deep as she was transported to heavenly realms through worship. The words of the song echoed the mediation of her heart as a product of a lifestyle of worship as she sang aloud, "In moments like these, I sing out a love song to Jesus"! How could she do that sitting in the back of a police car, beaten and bruised, wearing only the coat of her rescuer? The same way Paul and Silas sang from the darkest depth of the prison cell. They understood what it meant to be a true worshiper.

We Were Created for Worship

In the Old Testament, even those chosen by God turned their meditation to what they thought could benefit them at the moment. While Moses was on the mountaintop receiving the revelation of the Ten Commandments, which included "You shall have no other gods before me," the Israelites were gathering their gold to throw in the fire and create an object of worship. Their affections quickly turned from worshiping their Creator and Deliverer to worshiping an object created by their own hands.

We all worship. From pagans to devoted lovers of Jesus, we all worship something. God created us with a heart to worship. He created us to worship him. Yet, what we worship is determined by the meditation of our heart and how much of our time with the world we are willing to sacrifice for time with him. We can worship God and invite the kingdom of heaven into our lives, or we can worship the enemy and his world and invite the kingdom of evil into our lives. The choice is always ours. What and who we choose to worship and meditate on determines who we are. Just like you are what you eat, you are what you think. You are what you worship.

It is my hope and prayer that as you have followed me through my journey from abuse through recovery and on to abundant life and fruitful ministry, you have seen that this goes far beyond just a "tolerable recovery" or numb existence. God's plan for everyone is complete freedom and victory, and it is attainable for all with the courage and determination to make the journey. I hope that as you read these pages, your heart and your spirit have been touched, in whatever place you find yourself right now. I also pray that the words in this book have sparked hope in you and challenged you to reach for more in your life and your relationship with God. This book has been an absolute labor of love, and I hope it will help me proclaim the message of hope, healing, and complete restoration in Jesus Christ.

It is my prayer that as you apply the truths and challenges in this book, you may find the freedom for which you have been searching and that you will continue to strive to fulfill your greater purpose and destiny here on earth. In all things, may God richly bless you in your personal journey to live life empowered!

About the Author

Jadie grew up on the mission field in the islands of the South Pacific. There she learned the joys and blessings of serving God in ministry. She also learned the reality of bringing God's light to a fallen world as her family was violently attacked one dark night. Jesus said that we should expect tribulation in this world, but to take heart because he has overcome the world. She has experienced suffering and tribulation in body, soul, and spirit – but has learned the secrets of living as an overcomer through Christ. It is out of this that she now ministers hope for a new life to others as she speaks on forgiveness, hope, healing, spiritual authority, identity in Christ, marriage, and more.

Jadie has been married for 27 years and has four amazing kids. She has spent the past 25 years in ministry with her husband, leading in large churches, small churches, parachurch organizations, the military, and as Christian business owners. They are currently launching a new small-church movement in Northern Idaho focused on community and discipleship.